FAN
PHENOMENA

THE ROCKY HORROR
PICTURE SHOW

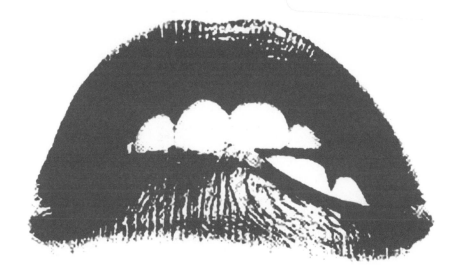

EDITED BY
MARISA C. HAYES

Credits

First published in the UK in 2015 by Intellect Books,
The Mill, Parnall Road, Fishponds, Bristol, BS16 3JG, UK

First published in the USA in 2015 by Intellect Books,
The University of Chicago Press, 1427 E. 60th Street,
Chicago, IL 60637, USA

Editor: Marisa C. Hayes

Series Editor and Design: Gabriel Solomons

Typesetting: Stephanie Sarlos

Copy Editor: Emma Rhys

A catalogue record for this book is available from
the British Library

Fan Phenomena Series
ISSN: 2051-4468
eISSN: 2051-4476

Fan Phenomena: The Rocky Horror Picture Show
ISBN: 978-1-78320-450-2
eISBN: 978-1-78320-451-9 / 978-1-78320-452-6

Printed and bound by
Bell & Bain Limited, Glasgow

Contents

Acknowledgements

I recall first viewing *The Rocky Horror Picture Show* on VHS with fondness, followed by live screenings and fan communities that allowed a bisexual 15-year-old theatre geek to fit in for once and have fun. For that, I'd like to thank my mother, a first generation *RHPS* fan, for showing me the film at just the right moment in my life. Not only did it provide comfort and entertainment, *RHPS* kindled a love of cinema that turned into a 'favourite obsession' and profession. Thanks are also due to the group of teenage misfits who accompanied me to my first live screenings, especially Ainslie, Amanda, Jessica, Jill and Jill's older sister, Jan (for providing transportation in a fabulous blue van).

I am grateful to the following people (in no particular order) who generously gave their time and support through interviews, consultations or editorial help with this volume: Fan Phenomena series editor Gabriel Solomons, Sal Piro, Ruth Fink-Winter, Stephanie Freeman, Larry Viezel, Shawn Stutler, Jim 'Cosmo' Hetzer, Bill Brennan, Malcolm Tay, my husband, and our cats for the love (but not the unwanted typos from streaking across the keyboard).

Last, but certainly not least, I'd like to express my appreciation for the book's contributors. Thank you for doing the 'Time Warp' with me!

Marisa C. Hayes, Editor

Introduction
Marisa C. Hayes

→ A long, long, time ago, in a galaxy far, far, away, God said, 'Let there be lips!'
And there were.
And they were good.

Any series on fan studies or cult cinema would be incomplete without a title exploring *The Rocky Horror Picture Show* (Jim Sharman, 1975), a film that not only helped shape, but also has come to define, the terms *audience participation, midnight movie* and *cult film*. No small feat given its initial lukewarm response, today *RHPS* is acknowledged as the film industry's longest-running theatrical release to date, complete with an international fan community that spans multiple generations. While the film's namesake will remain 'just 7 hours old' on-screen forever, the year 2015 marks the *The Rocky Horror Picture Show*'s 40th anniversary, a perfect time to re-examine and celebrate a veteran of fan phenomena that offered 'a different set of jaws' in 1975 and continues to expand its fandom with each passing decade.

The *RHPS* fandom, supported by both lifers (long-time fans, some of whom have been active since the film's release) and newbie 'creatures of the night', maintains a particularly active output that helps keep the community thriving, which is impressive given that its focus is a single film viewed as many as a thousand times or more by some fans. But *RHPS* is more than a film (although it *is* a good film contrary to outdated prejudices regarding genre films and B-movies that occasionally continue to plague critics), it is a universe that is still expanding, like Janet's mind.

Long-time fans are likely familiar with the history of Richard O'Brien's creation that debuted in 1973 on the London stage, directed by Jim Sharman (a production that, fittingly, Vincent Price is said to have attended). *The Rocky Horror Show* didn't add *Picture* to its title, of course, until the performance generated interest in a film version led by the same creative duo, as well as many members of the theatrical cast. The British/American co-production was filmed in England at Oakley Court/Bray Studios in 1974 and struggled at the box office a year later, despite successful stage runs on both sides of the Atlantic. It wasn't long, however, before the movie's midnight programming generated a celebrated new paradigm in filmgoing.

Frank-N-Furter's sung tribute to Fay Wray, 'how I started to cry / 'cause I wanted to be dressed just the same' proved to be prophetic as American audiences were the first to emulate their own *RHPS* screen (super)heroes whose proto-punk, glam-rock infused ensembles challenged traditional gender constructions and treated sexuality with a light-hearted playfulness. They weren't just passive observers, though; *RHPS* fans took the film's adage 'Don't dream it, be it' seriously, tapping into creative outlets to invent interactive dialogue, clever wordplay and use of props in a constantly evolving celebration of both community and individuality. And so it was that a film that began as a stage production regenerated a live experience around the globe through shadow casts and an unprecedented display of audience participation, an established term today thanks to the contributions of first-wave *RHPS* fans.

For many, the *RHPS* experience retains aspects of its early counterculture sensibilities by proposing liminal spaces that encourage playful yet poignant explorations of sexuality, gender and representation. Yet, despite its anything goes, non-conformist

Introduction
Marisa C. Hayes

reputation – or perhaps because of it, if the times are finally catching up to *RHPS* – the media has not let such an established icon of cult phenomena go unnoticed. As a result, *RHPS*'s 'unconventional conventionalists' have been infiltrating the mainstream, even as early as the late 1970s, while maintaining the fandom's unique qualities on their own terms. Recent examples range from an appearance by the Paris-based *Rocky* troupe, The Sweet Transvestites, on national television in France's *Got Talent* series, to the new 40th anniversary *RHPS* MAC cosmetics line, advertised as an 'orgy of colour'. The *RHPS* community at large seems to strike a positive balance between enjoying what such commercial ventures might offer while maintaining their own home-grown fandoms' inclusive and social atmosphere, something that has come to characterize the *RHPS* experience the world over, from Tel Aviv to Tokyo.

This community-driven fandom has resulted in recent projects like the crowd-funded documentary *Rocky Horror Saved My Life* (scheduled for release in late 2015) directed by Shawn Stutler or *The Rocky Horror Picture Book* (2014), a collection of Perry Bedden's behind-the-scenes photos that Jim 'Cosmo' Hetzer encouraged the celluloid Transylvanian to publish. Other cultural references outside the immediate *RHPS* fandom reflect not only the film's celebrated Dionysian flavour, but also its aforementioned inclusion. The two are joined, for example, in a recent review in *The Hollywood Reporter* that compares the rock opera-infused film *Peaches Does Herself* (created by the Berlin-based electro-punk pioneer Peaches in 2013) to *The Rocky Horror Picture Show* when referencing the artist's use of glam aesthetics and gender-fluid themes.

Further explorations of identity and representation are detailed in this book's chapters that address the film's characters and what playing them entails, including Tara Chittenden's 'Shadowing the Boss: Leadership and the Collective Creation of a Frank-N-Furter Identity in *Rocky Horror* Fan Casts'; Alissa Burger's 'Performing Promiscuity: Female Sexuality, Fandom and *The Rocky Horror Picture Show*'; as well as Sarah Cleary's fresh look at audience participation informed by her years of producing The Rocky Horror Picture Show Ireland in 'Don't Dream It, Be It: The Method in the Madness of *The Rocky Horror Picture Show*'. Shawn DeMille and Taos Glickman underline the sociopolitical aspects of the film's influence in 'Doing the Time Warp: Youth Culture, Coming of Age and *The Rocky Horror Picture Show* Through the Years'.

The film's iconic fashion, followed by the question of fan costumes and economics, are explored in Diana Heyne's 'Fashion and Fetish: *The Rocky Horror Picture Show*, Dark Cabaret Aesthetics and Proto-Punk' and Aubrey L. C. Mishou's 'Fishnet Economy: The Commerce of Costumes and *The Rocky Horror Picture Show*'. Other chapters cover additional areas of influence that examine the cultural currents running throughout *RHPS*, including a chapter by Molly McCourt entitled 'A Strange Journey: Finding Carnival in *The Rocky Horror Picture Show*', which provides an understanding of how Rabelais's sixteenth century French feasting and revelry is reappropriated and perpetuated in the film.

Additional contributions aimed at a better understanding of *RHPS*'s value as a cultural artefact include Franck Boulègue's 'Sanity for Today: Brad and Janet's Post-*Rocky Shock Treatment*', a chapter dedicated to *RHPS*'s ill-fated sequel that contextualizes *Rocky*'s success through the lens of Richard O'Brien and Jim Sharman's second lesser-known screen collaboration. Reuben C. Oreffo's 'Philosophical Currents Through Film' applies the analytic philosophy tradition to explore aspects of *RHPS*, including language and representation, while Andrew Howe studies how *RHPS* uprooted a number of deep-seated western traditions in 'Mercy Killing: *Rocky Horror*, the Loss of Innocence and the Death of Nostalgia'.

Whether you appreciate it for being the first pastiche film to honour Hammer Horror, vintage sci-fi and musicals; for its queering of the cinematic space; for the camaraderie of its community; or for a myriad of reasons including all of the above, I hope you enjoy the intelligent yet entertaining chapters that follow in celebration of *The Rocky Horror Picture Show*'s ongoing fascination and success. May they keep you all shivering with antici...SAY IT...pation, preferably whilst wearing a feather boa and a load of sequins! ●

~~~~~~~~~

GO FURTHER

Online

The Rocky Horror Picture Show: The Official Fan Site: http://www.rockyhorror.com/

Rockypedia: http://www.rockypedia.org/Rockypedia

Chapter
01

Fashion and Fetish: *The Rocky Horror Picture Show*, Dark Cabaret Aesthetics and Proto-Punk

Diana Heyne

→ Manifestations of alternative culture or Bohemianism in fashion have worn many faces over the years, inspired by a desire to celebrate the qualities of uniqueness, creativity and individual freedom rather than rest unnoticed in the safety of the mainstream fold. Alternative fashion is also one of the most highly visible means of social and political provocation available, but as such requires periodic renewal to retain its attention-getting power.

In this most telling badge of membership in another realm, fashion amongst the hip has relied on a spirit of creative change and rebellion, even against its own ranks, in order to retain momentum and keep the deadening forces of ennui at bay. Borrowing a cue from physics, one might even posit that for every alternative fashion action there is an equal and opposite reaction; as looks evolve from one 'movement' into another they often embrace the polar opposite of their predecessors, to which society at large has become gradually acclimated. This framework of cyclic evolution provides one lens to examine the fashion and cultural influences that shaped the style of *The Rocky Horror Picture Show* and, conversely, how its inspirational fashion energy helped to create some of the defining looks of 1970s alternative and popular culture, participating particularly in the genesis and eventual international style dissemination of punk and its less astringent, romantic sibling New Wave.

If hippie fashion of the late 1960s and early 1970s looked to a natural, earthy aesthetic of ethnic cotton, peasant-style embroideries, faded denim and long, unstyled hair for both sexes, offering a celebration of nature centred, agrarian cultures around the globe, the look that evolved in alternative culture at the very end of hippiedom was in many ways its antithesis. The punk culture that burgeoned during the 1970s celebrated anarchy through its street-smart urban dress of slashed T-shirts, laddered fishnets and safety pin piercings as well as borrowing heavily from then lesser-known specialty fashions like the corsets, extreme stiletto heels and latex garb of fetishists and drag queens, among others. The 1960s had opened the Pandora's box of free love; the 1970s wanted to explore the previously shadowy margins of desire, and alternative fashion reflected this urge.

In this transitional period of the early to mid-1970s, *Rocky Horror* was present as an alternative fashion force, setting trends but more especially diffusing them, from its beginnings as a London stage show through its distribution as a film available to an international audience. In this era prior to cable television, music video channels and the Internet, the uniquely blended anarchy of nostalgia, fetish dress, drag glamour and cosplay inspiration that is *Rocky Horror* became a prime instigator in the widespread change that would eventually propel the styles of first-wave punk, New Wave and proto-Goth into an international spotlight.

The Rocky Horror Picture Show posited anything but naturalism; it presented a fashion aesthetic drawn from the secret worlds of the imagination, of the unbridled id expressed in sexual anarchy and fetishism, with inspiration drawn from mid-twentieth-century horror and science fiction married to rock and roll. The look was studied, corseted and manufactured: make-up, hair colour and style were obviously artificial, a careful construct that clearly denoted the wearer's tongue-in-cheek, oddly menacing otherness. Dark glamour and sequins edged out natural fabrics; kitsch was celebrated and the cynical edge of urban civilization, always on the brink of potential catastrophe, overruled the naïve desire to return to an archetypal paradise garden. This was fashion

Fashion and Fetish:
The Rocky Horror Picture Show, **Dark Cabaret Aesthetics and Proto-Punk**
Diana Heyne

with a confrontational edge and grittiness the likes of which had not been previously available for widespread consumption. At this remove, it is almost difficult to imagine the full aesthetic shock-value that *The Rocky Horror Picture Show* possessed during its first years of release, since so much of the look has been assimilated into popular culture, yet *RHPS* still possesses a classic alternative fashion appeal that is a tribute to the film's pioneering creativity and unrestricted sensual energy.

Sue Blane, costume designer for both the stage and film versions of *Rocky Horror,* has been credited by some as a prime force behind the punk look that originated in 1970s London. In an interview that first appeared in the publication *Crazed Imaginations #84* in August 2002, Blane was asked by writer Ruth Fink-Winter:

Ruth Fink-Winter: Patricia Quinn says that you invented punk. What do you think about that?
Sue Blane: There's no question that the punk look was about in London on the streets, and I was drawing on that. But what I added to it was the ripped fishnets, the sequins glued on, the whole distressing idea, plus I think the fun of it... So whether I invented punk, I don't know, but I'm very happy Pat Quinn says I did. If one can be proud of something like that!

Then Blane goes on to explain that:

Malcolm McClaren [*sic*] and Vivienne Westwood had a bit to do with it as well... certainly I was drawing on all that. I owe a lot to them in that respect. In fact, Magenta's wonderful little spiky boots that she wore with the spacesuit came from 'Granny Takes a Trip' [*Crazed Imaginations* ed. note: McClaren's (*sic*) and Westwood's shop that later became 'Sex']. One of our totally over-the-top purchases with our very small budget... We remade them for the movie.

This pointy-toed, fetish-inspired look in footwear selected by Blane certainly became an iconic, long-lived and much-beloved style among those of the punk, Goth and New Wave persuasions.

In her *Crazed Imaginations* interview Blane also elaborates on how corsets, another look that would become a punk and New Wave standard, came to feature so intrinsically in the signature *Rocky Horror* style, stating that she had previously costumed Tim Curry in a production of Jean Genet's *The Maids,* staged by Lindsay Kemp in 1971 at Glasgow's Citizens' Theatre. Blane credits Kemp's vision of dark cabaret, transexuality and gay theatre as guiding forces in developing the costuming for the Genet work and explains that she herself went on to build on this aesthetic for the costuming of *Rocky Horror,* even going so far as to borrow Tim Curry's original corset from *The Maids.* Here Blane has clearly established the cabaret/drag queen standard, one of the iconic looks of punk, Goth and New Wave: underwear as outerwear, in particular the corset as a fashion 'must have', in a lineage that descends (and becomes increasingly commercialized) through Madonna's skilful exploitation of the concept, to the contemporary manipulations of Lady Gaga.

Blane's work in costuming Genet hints at the alternative cultural forces at work at *Rocky Horror*'s inception, forces that were to influence the androgyny present in punk and New Wave style overall, as the gay liberation movement that emerged during the late 1960s continued to gain momentum throughout the decade of the 1970s. Gay culture and drag cabaret in particular certainly provided the inspiration for important nuances of the costuming that was being explored by glam rockers like David Bowie or the New York Dolls, and was an integral part of the look that set *The Rocky Horror Picture Show* in a sexually ambivalent realm of its own. Alongside the send-up of the more flamboyant aspects of drag culture present in *The Rocky Horror Picture Show*, there are also more sobering references to gay history: Frank-N-Furter's pink triangle-adorned surgical scrubs co-opt the symbol used by the Nazis to mark homosexuals, a symbol that was later transmuted by gay activists into a positive acknowledgement of their identity.

In regarding the other eclectic sources that informed Blane, propelled *The Rocky Horror Picture Show* and stimulated the fashion world of punk and New Wave, it is impossible to overlook the effect of mid-twentieth-century classic films, especially horror and science fiction. In a world pre-Internet, home video/DVD players and cable television, films shown in theatres were perhaps the most accessible and influential visual links to the fashion of earlier eras, whether portraying historic styles or those of imagined realms. In the 1970s repertory art cinemas grew in number and popularity, mixing alternative films with vintage classics at an appealing price, offering a source of inspiration and ready access to a showcase of aesthetic styles from the past, one that often changed nightly with the swiftly rotated films. The world of cinematic theatre was ripe to inspire, share and promote, and *The Rocky Horror Picture Show* reaped the benefits from each of these aspects, first for its own creative formation, and second, from having precisely the sort of venues needed to become a participatory cult success and international source of style inspiration.

Theatrical rock and rollers like David Bowie, taking a fashion cue from the feminine glamour in many vintage films, initially began to flaunt a nostalgically clothed transgender style which for Bowie soon evolved into a series of looks that were literally alien in character. On the cover of his *Aladdin Sane* album (1973), resembling nothing less than an androgynous extraterrestrial, Bowie was an avant-garde head turner at the time of the LP's release and certainly provided ample inspiration to slightly later fashion ventures like *The Rocky Horror Picture Show* and punk styles in hair and make-up. During the early 1970s, Bowie continually mined the science fiction/extraterrestrial vein for entire concept albums and the looks that went with them, such as his Ziggy Stardust persona. It was a look that *Rocky Horror* and punk culture would embrace and exploit,

Fashion and Fetish:
***The Rocky Horror Picture Show*, Dark Cabaret Aesthetics and Proto-Punk**
Diana Heyne

although *The Rocky Horror Picture Show* also draws directly on the kitsch costuming of vintage science fiction and horror films like *Flash Gordon* (Frederick Stephani & Ray Taylor, 1936) and *The Bride of Frankenstein* (James Whale, 1935) for outfits such as Riff Raff and Magenta's visually striking space suits, and her coiffure at the film's conclusion.

While it would be overly simplistic to credit *Rocky Horror*'s fashion influence with the invention of punk style (since clearly any alternative fashion movement is the result of multiple influences, including some concepts built upon the alternative culture that proceeded them but also embracing the destruction of earlier fashion aesthetics with a visual polar shift); however, if *The Rocky Horror Picture Show* was not the sole pro- genitor of these styles, it was most certainly among the guiding lights to punk and New Wave fashion. *Rocky Horror* achieved this status with a mix of quirky originality that was diffused through film's then unrivalled ability to disseminate style at a larger-than- life scale. In the 1970s, at a time when today's contemporary plethora of virtual visual stimuli did not exist, cinema (as discussed earlier) was a lively force in heralding fashion change, reaching an audience that the limited number of television networks and their basically conservative stance could not.

Beyond the more obvious impact of *The Rocky Horror Picture Show*, retained by viewers in visual and emotional memory – witness the mounting anticipation among early audiences as Frank descended in the elevator and that shared gasp when it was finally seen what sort of beautifully perverse creature stepped out of the cage, unfurling himself from a cloak straight out of Dracula's closet – there is the culturally significant birth of the phenomenon of audience participation. *The Rocky Horror Picture Show*'s well-defined and not taxingly difficult-to-replicate looks facilitated these forays into nascent cosplay; a simple collection of items carried enough symbolic weight to be- come shorthand for a character: Frank requires little more than a corset and garters,

heavily layered eye make-up and a heart tattoo; Eddie, a leather biker vest and jeans, pomaded hair and a comb; neither too difficult or costly to procure, but instantly recognizable. Audience members were invited not just to fantasize, but become, and they took quite literally to the film's challenge. The legacy of *The Rocky Horror Picture Show* was multiplied exponentially when audience participation stepped in. Audience members were (and still are) challenged to investigate their own creativity within the parameters of a guiding template, and their treasure hunts for costume parts frequently took them exploring through thrift shops and dusty attics. Many of them discovered it was the foundation of a look they could carry happily into life outside the theatre. In a world where Halloween was for children under twelve and costume parties few and far between, *The Rocky Horror Picture Show* answered a need to be different and fulfilled the love of dressing up that so many fans have revelled in over the ensuing years. Even the contemporary manifestations of various cosplay conventions outside the *Rocky Horror* universe owe a great debt to that simple exhortation: 'Don't dream it, be it'.

Whether *The Rocky Horror Picture Show* was an original instigator or acted as a promotional conduit, the eclecticism that is an *RHPS* fashion tenet was also embraced by the alternative fashion styles of punk and New Wave. *Rocky Horror* provided an appealingly varied catalogue of inspirational choice drawn from historical dress, established fantasy and free imagination. One could borrow from any or several of these to create looks that astonished, selectively offended or questioned the logic of mainstream culture; especially significant since much of first-wave punk ideology revolved around the idea of anarchy and street confrontation via style.

While Frank's eye-catching lingerie-clad look and beautifully made-up face are the stylistic visual focus of much of the film, other characters brought equally influential fashion details to *RHPS*, and into the field of play during the initial burgeoning of punk and New Wave. Memorable and recognizable examples of this influence are alive and well today, and though no longer brave new looks, are still powerful enough to rest outside the comfort zone of most of mainstream culture.

While at first glance eyebrows might seem a relatively secondary feature, in reality Columbia's brows, camouflaged and re-drawn a la Marlene Dietrich (channelled via gay cabaret) provided immediately visible verification of otherness. This created or drawn brow remains an attention getter capable of remaking the appearance of an entire face, and was often employed during the punk era in make-up designs that pushed the boundaries of human appearance, the more extreme creating illusions that also relocated other features entirely. The thin-line eyebrow is still much in evidence today, touted by the likes of Gothic dreamers, neo-punks and alternative performers such as Amanda Palmer. Addi-

Fashion and Fetish:
The Rocky Horror Picture Show, **Dark Cabaret Aesthetics and Proto-Punk**
Diana Heyne

Figure 3: Magenta taking a cue from silent film 'vamp' style © Twentieth Century Fox.

tionally, Columbia's intensely red-dyed, boy-cut hair in *The Rocky Horror Picture Show* is both androgynous and visibly faux. It signalled a thumbs-up to fantasy hairstyles after the constraining naturalism of the late 1960s, revelling in the anti-naturalism and imaginative possibilities of hair dyes as well as elevating to new popularity a previously reviled hair colour that had long deserved a return to the revered status it held in the nineteenth century (those with naturally red hair went during this period from being mercilessly teased 'carrot tops' to objects of envy and desire, like the nineteenth century Pre-Raphaelite painter Rossetti's ginger 'stunners'). From the neck down, Columbia's vintage movie-musical inspired sequined tap suit or burlesque corset and boa have inspired punk/New Wave costume accessories and become staples that are perhaps more popular than ever in contemporary alternative burlesque theatre.

Magenta's iconic punk footwear was not the only style-setting look provided by this character. The halo of hennaed hair, white face, heavily kohl-rimmed eyes and profoundly red lips sported by Magenta offered a slightly more sinister, vampiric take on vintage film style, recalling the publicity photos of silent film star and 'vamp', Theda Bara.

Magenta's languidly sexy black-negligee dinner attire, black stockings and intentionally displayed garters are aspects of cabaret/burlesque style that set enduring and much beloved examples for punk and New Wave. The fact that until the film's end, along with others like Riff Raff and the Transylvanians, Magenta is always clad in black, foreshadows the trend to dress entirely in sombre tones that would dominate much of hipster style in the late 1970s and the 1980s, making black the prime colour of choice for many punks, New Wavers and naturally, Goths.

Eddie's 1950s-inspired love of high-reaching hair, leather and leopard-skin prints

Figure 4: Brad and Janet in 1960s costume © Twentieth Century Fox.

dubs him a herald of the revival of earlier rebellious styles, mimicking the English Teddy Boys and American 'greasers'. Eddie's style found resonance in alternative cultural exploration of 1950s Rockabilly fashion and music during the 1970s and 1980s, and at that time established its enduring place among the range of fashion looks that were and are alt-culture standards.

Even those uncool kids, science-class sweethearts Brad and Janet, whose dress and attitudes hark back to straight culture of the early 1960s, had their stylistic revenge in the nerdiness transmuted to cool espoused by the likes of 1970s and 1980s alternative music icons, such as Elvis Costello and Talking Heads front man David Byrne, who became style setters to be emulated. This celebration of geekiness is an impulse that has endured and evolved, contributing to the fashion style present in contemporary nerd culture, where horn-rimmed glasses and plaid have become a popular badge of honour.

Of Riff Raff it can be said in particular that his black, fingerless gloves, or mitts, with their echoes of Victoriana and Dickensian street waifs, would become one of the defining accessories for the era of punk and New Wave. They were an ever-present accessory in alternative circles, whether on the street, or in clubs, where they could be seen on both musicians and audience. Mitts certainly remain a popular style accessory with alternative culture darlings, and are today accepted in their many forms among even the less fashionably daring. An Internet search currently turns up literally hundreds of photographs of examples of fingerless gloves for sale.

The charting of cultural influences is never an exact science, especially in the world of cutting-edge fashion; so many energies come into play, yet *The Rocky Horror Picture Show* clearly has been and remains an influential force, one that had an undoubted role in shaping the long-lived styles of punk, New Wave and Goth culture. *The Rocky Horror*

Fashion and Fetish:
The Rocky Horror Picture Show, **Dark Cabaret Aesthetics and Proto-Punk**
Diana Heyne

Figure 5: Riff Raff in his Victorian 'street waif'-style fingerless gloves © Twentieth Century Fox.

Picture Show brought a radically different vision of fashion to the masses sitting in the dark of mid-1970s theatres outside the punk epicentres of London and New York. It assisted in transfusing a dose of creative life, and even hope, into a world poised awkwardly between Woodstock and *Saturday Night Fever* (John Badham, 1977), between tie-dye T-shirts and polyester suits. There was an alternative fashion hero outside the realms of the faded denim tried-and-true or the inauspiciously conceived synthetic new, and he was wearing a corset, fishnets and platform heels and making randy sacrifice before a deity named Charles Atlas... ●

~~~~~~~~~~

GO FURTHER

Books

The Rocky Horror Picture Show (Cultographies)
Jeffrey Weinstock
(London/New York: Wallflower Press, 2007)

Online

'Sue Blane Interview – Crazed Imaginations'
Interview by Ruth Fink-Winter
Rockypedia.org (n.d. [2002]), http://www.rockypedia.org/Sue_Blane_Interview_-_Crazed_Imaginations.
[Adapted from *Crazed Imaginations* #84, where it originally appeared.]

'Exclusive Interview: Sue Blane'
Interview by Patricia Morrisroe
RockyMusic.org (n.d. [1979]), http://www.rockymusic.org/showdoc/SueBlane-1979Interview.php.

Fan Appreciation no.1
Sal Piro, President RHPS Fan Club

Interview by Marisa C. Hayes

Marisa C. Hayes (MCH): *We know that* RHPS *has an amazing capacity to regenerate itself through shadow casts and other tribute shows, inspiring different types of performances, but how has* RHPS *influenced the other characters or drag performances you incarnate?*

Sal Piro (SP): I had already been involved with *Rocky* for over ten years before I started working out at Fire Island [New York]. When I performed in the early days of *Rocky* in the theatres, I did mostly comic take-offs on Janet, Riff Raff, Rocky, etc. At Fire Island when I became entertainment director of the Ice Palace, a huge club which featured drag, I did mostly comic take-offs of Mama Cass, Madonna and Dame Edna. My experience at Rocky certainly had an effect on my performances.

MCH: *Speaking of roles, as long-time president of the RHPS Fan Club,* Creatures of the Night [1990] *author, and having represented the fandom on-screen in a number of feature films and documentaries (from your cameo in* Shock Treatment [Jim Sharman, 1981] *to* Fame [Alan Parker, 1980], *among others), being a fan has turned into a role itself and you're legendary among us unconventional conventionalists. Did you ever imagine that it would lead to this?*

SP: I just remember the early days of going to *RHPS*. How I loved the movie so much, really loved the soundtrack, and in the early days standing in line for 3–4 hours with other fans and forming this community. I guess you would say it all came from our mutual interest and love of the film/music. We loved it so much we wanted to be part of it and thus the audience participation evolved from the passion we had for the movie.

MCH: *You've published two volumes of* Creatures of the Night *and soon* The Rocky Horror Treasury *will be released, attesting to how important Rocky remains for fans from all walks of life. What do you think of the growing number of film critics that claim RHPS is no longer 'transgressive' or that it's just a rite of passage for adolescents?*

SP: I would say, consider the adults who went in their youth and still love the film today, bringing their friends, family, children, and eventually their grandchildren. More than just a rite of passage… more of a STATE OF MIND.

MCH: *What's next for Sal Piro? And the fan club?*

Fan Appreciation no. 1
Sal Piro

SP: What's next... *Rocky* continues in the electronic/social media age... the word gets out so much faster now. Next September/October we will be celebrating the 40th Anniversary of the release of the film. New products. New releases. *Rocky*'s own make-up line (MAC)... and a celebration to outdo them all!!!!!

SP: *And one last question (that I can't resist): as a competitive* Scrabble *tournament player, has the chance to spell a winning Rocky-related word ever come up?*

SP: I have actually played the word R-O-C-K-Y many times and the word H-O-R-R-O-R... but never in the same game. ●

‘WHATEVER HAPPENED TO SATURDAY NIGHT? WHEN YOU DRESSED UP SHARP AND YOU FELT ALRIGHT.’

EDDIE

Chapter
02

Doing the Time Warp: Youth Culture, Coming-of-Age and *The Rocky Horror Picture Show* Through the Years

Taos Glickman and Shawn DeMille

→ *Rocky Horror* coming(-of-age)
One recurring question comes to mind when discussing *The Rocky Horror Picture Show:* why do audiences keep watching what ostensibly should be at best (on merits alone) just an entertaining, salacious B-movie? Moreover, why would youth flock to midnight showings of this film with shadow casts for four decades now?

What is it about a man in fishnets, an 'asshole' in his undies and a pair of elbow-sex-giving siblings, that makes them come back time and time again? These are all important questions that lead to the same conclusion: *Rocky Horror* is a coming-of-age experience for both the characters *and* the audience. *RHPS* brings a queer worldview to the forefront of people's hearts and minds, and allows them to contribute to social change by their participation in the 'Don't dream it, be it' philosophy.

Giving language to identity
Prior to *Rocky Horror* people who were gender-transgressive were often called 'transvestites'. They identified as men but dressed up as women, usually part-time. These 'trans' individuals were a major part of the (1969) Stonewall Riots and would later choose to be identified as 'drag queens', taking the Shakespearean stage direction of 'drag' (dressed as a girl) and playing with the idea of gender as a performative act.

To those for whom gender was more than just a nightlife act but instead an identity that resulted from being born with the 'wrong' sex organs, words like 'transsexual' were not in the common parlance, even amongst the burgeoning gay community forming at the time. Their overwhelming absence from media depictions rendered the community essentially invisible to society, or what media theorist George Gerbner would call 'symbolically annihilated'. The

Figure 1: Life at midnight before The Rocky Horror Picture Show, The Stonewall Inn, '69 © StatisSquareSpace.

ability to see oneself represented in popular culture is psychologically powerful and important. Ultimately, *RHPS* emboldened this nascent 'hearts and minds' revolution towards a new era of gay visibility.

As it looks towards the future, the film also uses symbols to reflect on queer history, notably the pink triangle on Frank-N-Furter's surgery gown, or the rainbow colours that Rocky's tank takes on before he is 'born'. Their use sends a subtler message to the audience that queerness was not always celebrated. The pink triangle is a reference to the Holocaust, when gay and gender non-conforming individuals were sent to camps and ghettos, forced to wear the triangle on their clothes, just as Jews were required to wear the yellow Star of David.

Yet this subversive reference does not darken the tone of the film, but instead demonstrates how careful the LGBTQ community had to be prior to the '*Rocky* era'. Conventions like the one hosted at the castle were usually held in secret, which is why Brad

**Doing the Time Warp: Youth Culture,
Coming-of-Age and *The Rocky Horror Picture Show* Through the Years**
Taos Glickman and Shawn DeMille

*Figure 2: Frank-N-Furter
snaps a glove while wearing
his gown with the Pink Triangle © Twentieth Century Fox.*

and Janet were forced into the castle after discovering that it was taking place. In real life, these were legitimate fears about being 'outed' because the gay community was fraught with an immense fear of being discovered and ending up dead or excommunicated, simply for expressing their most authentic selves. This is why these messages remain so powerful, even decades later. The symbols once used so hatefully, are now associated with acceptance. The LGBTQ community has reclaimed them to erase their dark meaning and instead create a new message of hope. Importantly, the collective memory is not forgotten; *Rocky Horror* houses it for future generations to reflect upon as they experience the film.

Subverting heteronormativity:
Safe-space sexuality

The Rocky Horror Picture Show is never apologetic in its use of sexuality. Frank-N-Furter tries just as hard to get into Janet's panties as he does Brad's briefs (and only succeeds with the latter, but hey, not even Frank-N-Furter can bat a perfect game). Normalizing this gender-variance creates a safe space in *Rocky Horror* within which identity can be explored. The film stands in as a coming-of-age experience not just for Brad and Janet, but for the audience as well. Through the unwavering acceptance of its queer self, the film gives words and purpose to an idea that was barely forming at the time: that being part of the LGBTQ community was OK. That one can be sexual and transgressive, and still be safe.

This is further examined with Rocky himself, Dr Frank-N-Furter's creation of an idealized sexual partner. Even though he is just 7 hours old, (and of course, truly beautiful to behold), Rocky also comes-of-age in the film. The twist is that his coming-of-age/coming-out process is reversed from the expected norm: first he grapples with homosexual, followed by heterosexual, encounters. Thus, Rocky is transgressive by exploring his possible heterosexuality in the film, which turns the filmic expectation of heteronormativity upside down. It renders heterosexuality the anomaly. Rocky is allowed to explore his sexuality in an accepting environment (even if it does cause jealousy between Frank-N-Furter *and* Janet). Even Rocky's final act is meant to demonstrate the queerness of the film's characters and their approach towards open sexuality. As Rocky ascends the RKO Tower with Dr Frank-N-Furter, he is referencing the movie *King Kong* (Cooper & Schoedsack, 1933), or rather re-referencing, since Fay Wray was already brought up earlier in the scene. In doing so, Rocky becomes the ape that kidnaps his beautiful lady. This act demonstrates how much we as the audience are supposed to interact with Rocky as a creature that can love a woman or a man, not forced to live within the confines of

Figure 3: Columbia, Riff Raff
and Magenta dance in front
of the rainbow tank from
which Rocky emerged ©
Twentieth Century Fox.

heterosexually preordained norms. As the movie also became a live-show experience, this anti-homophobic worldview expanded.

    The Rocky Horror Picture Show, more often than not, is viewed as part of a larger experience with a shadow cast. This entails re-enacting the scenes of the movie for an audience that is also participating in the experience, constructing a new narrative that has its own lexicon, and forms a community of practice. Part of what is most important in the *RHPS* experience is, of course, audience participation. Without this participation, the film loses some of its wonder and playful power. Audience participation is what transforms *Rocky Horror* from mere camp pastiche to the pansexual celebratory movement it is today. Attendants participate in an environment free from judgement. Moreover, younger viewers, teenagers and young adults, are immersed in a world that was created by those who came before. At the same time, the *Rocky* world evolves with each new audience and generation that comes through.

Don't dream it, be it

'Don't dream it, be it' was Dr Frank-N-Furter's (played by English actor Tim Curry) prescription for his queer-embracing generation and beyond. Not content to simply watch, the audience wanted to get involved in both the pageantry and the message it represented. 'Don't dream it, be it', is not just a call for more males in fishnets and platform heels, but a powerful harbinger of social change. Social change requires mass-participation – and perhaps a floorshow. *Rocky Horror* was released less than a decade after the 1969 Stonewall Riots in New York City, which provided a call-to-action for the Gay Rights Movement as queer individuals protested their homophobic treatment and police targeting after a raid on the queer-catering establishment. Films can provide impetus for change, like the foundational 1970 play-turned-cinematic release, *The Boys in the Band* (William Friedkin), which attempted to chronicle authentic gay male life and was already groundbreaking in its endeavour to humanize the gay experience. At the same time, society was reimagining the sexual, civil and gender rights of the individual. Artist Andy Warhol's 'Factory' aesthetics during the 1960s alongside musical movements, such as British glam rock and American adherents like Lou Reed, further increased queer visibility in popular culture during the early 1970s. As a whole, these various artists and films introduced queer sensibilities to society in a new, more open way.

The Rocky Horror Pictures Show played its part in this LGBTQ-rooted social change by displaying queer sexuality as explicit and normalized within the filmic space. Furthermore, it critiqued traditional American puritanical sexual repression and heterosexist assumptions, in effect turning them upside down. To this end, the film displays gender ambiguity and the pansexual use of drag, what could be called 'macho-drag' in which both traditionally masculine *and* feminine aspects become equally lust-worthy. Not surprisingly, the film itself is cloaked in safe-space film genres.

Rocky Horror and its genre references

Infusing this gender-blurring tale of transvestites from another planet is the genre-blurring content of horror, science fiction, the musical and gay 'camp'. The transatlantic lineage of the participatory screenings of *The Rocky Horror Picture Show* emerged with red lips from the American studio-era of the 1920s–1950s, sometimes referred to as Classical Hollywood Cinema (CHC). Brad and Janet are caricatures of the traditional CHC screen couple: heterosexual and celibate until marriage. *RHPS* reimagines this G-rated CHC fixation on marriage and coupling in favour of eroticism and fluidity of sexuality, with an added sadistic flourish for leather and whips.

Genre, from the Latin word 'genus', which means 'kind', 'stock' or 'birth', strives towards coherence-creating and linguistically-organizing principles. Particularly within a CHC framework, film theorists like Rick Altman echoed this linguistic approach explaining that linguistic and textual methods combine; theory combines with history. Furthermore, Thomas Schatz, in his seminal 1981 text *Hollywood Genres*, discussed how a genre film is, '[o]ne which involves familiar, essentially one-dimensional characters acting out a predictable story pattern within a familiar setting'. Ultimately, genres help predetermine that there will be a presence of 'limited contexts' based on previously-used content and conventions. At the same time, this condensing of narrative depth means an increased likelihood of commonalties and consistencies will emerge for evaluation. Specifically within *Rocky Horror*, the genres at play are science fiction, horror and the musical.

RHPS features musical numbers throughout, including a 1930s Busby Berkeley-inspired floorshow with a kaleidoscope of bodies. Additionally, it is arguable that *RHPS* is a drag version and amalgamation of 1950s Hollywood horror and especially science fiction films, fixated on sexual practices. Within the horror genre, Dr Frankenstein becomes Frank-N-Furter, to Rocky's blonde and bronzed monster. Additionally, Rocky Horror firmly entrenches itself in the science fiction genre with the title song, 'Science Fiction/Double Feature'. Within this genre space, once Brad and Janet enter Dr Frank-N-Furter's realm, traditional heterosexual and marriage norms are 'alien' objects for dismantling. The science fiction genre often includes fantasy and imaginative elements. This encourages political and social expression that contemporary culture is often unwilling to accept. For example, whether it was an interracial kiss in 1960s *Star Trek* (Gene Roddenberry), or an allegory for the dangers of an un-critiqued focus on communism in *The Twilight Zone* (Rod Serling), science fiction remains a consistent host for social critique.

Moreover, the *RHPS* practice of dressing up as characters and bringing movie props to screenings is akin to other science fiction forms of 'cosplay', such as *Star Trek*'s 'Trekkies', and *Star Wars* or *Dr Who*-crowded convention halls. *RHPS* even ends with both a science fiction and horror motif: 'Someday, we shall return'. Horror, science fiction and the musical all presuppose experimental and sometimes provocative content. However, within these genres there is also a gay 'camp' reading influenced by the 'Theatre of the Ridiculous', an acting style popular in the 1960s and 1970s in England and the United States.

Theatre of the Ridiculous delighted in exaggeration and gender-bending. This is illuminated in other films such as those by Andy Warhol, and post-1960s readings of films like the American marijuana melodrama *Reefer Madness* (Louis Gasnier, 1936). Overall, Theatre of the Ridiculous focused on humour and hypocrisy, which frames popular notions of 'camp'. Celebrated cultural critic Susan Sontag's 1964 'Notes on Camp' included an amalgamated definition of 'camp' in film as a particular style and aesthetic drawn towards the details of absurdity and artifice, especially in the CHC period; a period very much played on in *Rocky Horror*.

Youth and coming-of-age

While these various genres texturize the reading of *The Rocky Horror Picture Show*, it is young audiences decade after decade that keep the message of 'Don't dream it, be it' alive. Easier acceptance of reimagining social practices in society is more commonly associated with youth because they are still in the process of forming their identities. Adolescence and young adulthood is a critical time for an individual to synthesize both group and personal identity, especially one with positive group interactions, also known as social competency. All of these issues intersect in the audience participation and coming-of-age story of *RHPS*.

Brad and Janet represent sexually traditional puritanical practices, along with their teacher and mentor Dr Scott. Furthermore, Dr Scott is rendered even more sexually repressed, through his literal impotence from paralysis. As Dr Frank-N-Furter's nemesis, Dr Scott provides a strong dramatic foil to all of Frank-N-Furter's sexual 'debauchery'. Along these lines, it is noted that the audience participation screenings of *RHPS* add dialogue and props throughout the film without disparagement of the content, but rather with acceptance, familiarity and bawdy humorous affection for it. The audience sides with the sexually experimental, over older, more traditional notions. Just as Brad and Janet come-of-age in absolute pleasure during the film, so too have young audiences over the years.

**Doing the Time Warp: Youth Culture,
Coming-of-Age and *The Rocky Horror Picture Show* Through the Years**
Taos Glickman and Shawn DeMille

The generational gap

In the 1970s the Gay Rights Movement, was still nascent and ripe for articulation. Accordingly, *Rocky*'s teenage consortium was ready-made for this emerging realm. Whether it was a new cross-dressing experience, or doing the *Time Warp* with a group of strangers, *RHPS*'s audience flourished around self-expression and discovery. Among the first to experience the shadow cast were teen *Rocky* fans born during the Baby Boom Generation (a period that spans the end of World War II to the early 1960s), just like Dr Frank-N-Furter himself (Tim Curry was born in 1946). This group can be called the 'First Wave' of Frank-N-Furter's children. While older folks were free to roam the midnight seats as well, adolescents and young adults had the greatest biological and psychological imperatives to explore and form identity. Just as the Gay Rights Movement was burgeoning, so too were the lives of these Baby Boomer adolescents. After the Stonewall Riots in 1969, early mobilizing organizations were formed like the Gay Liberation Front (GLF), and the Gay Activist Alliance in 1970. Additionally, there were increased articles in such publications as the *Village Voice* and new queer journalistic outlets like 1970's *Come Out*. These titles used media to politicize and dramatize the increasing 'Gay Power Movement', or what one historian called a media focus on gay 'dramatic street theatre'.

The Rocky Horror Picture Show as an extension of this momentum allowed youth to perform this same 'theatre' style indoors and at the midnight hour. For the audience, the modern Post-Stonewall Gay Rights Movement was still in its infancy. *RHPS* created a safe space when so many other places outside of its (Great Scott!) toilet-papered walls were not. 'Don't dream it, be it', was a wonderful fantasy for many GLBTQ and allies during the 1970s, but few could see it actualized in the non-*Rocky* world. *Rocky Horror*'s power for social change was allowing the audience to see young people on the screen and stage who were gay, straight and anything in-between, realize their sexuality and identity openly, safely and positively. Audiences could come-of-age with Brad and Janet, 'don't dream it, be it' stuck in their heads and hearts, longing to see this change in the real world.

'Don't dream it, be it' took on a new sentiment for Generation X's *Rocky* teens, born roughly in the mid-1960s to late 1970s. These 'Second Wave' *Rocky* fans went to the *RHPS* in the 1980s and 1990s. At that point, Gay Rights had a more established platform, and a mobilizing issue in the form of HIV/AIDS. Yet the safe space of *RHPS* was still needed for out-and-proudness because it was also a buffer from the sexual caution and moral panic of the time. Gay lifestyles had long been placed at the fringes of American as well as British life and popular culture. However, fears of HIV/AIDS, overwhelmingly focused on the gay community especially in the 1980s, put *Rocky*-styled displays of mass-sexuality in a further predicament. By 1986 the first national HIV/AIDS awareness campaign, 'Don't Die of Ignorance' was launched in the United Kingdom, as well as a public acknowledgement by US President Ronald Regan that AIDS research and discus-

Figure 4: The progeny (must)
move on. A classic Rocky audience, New York © Tumblr.

sion should be a national priority.

In this framework, *Rocky Horror* was no longer just composed of a series of genres playing with the idea of sexuality in society. Rather, *Rocky* fulfilled a coming-of-
age need for sexuality among Generation X in general. If Brad, Janet and Rocky could
express their emerging desires, so too could Generation X. They could imagine what
they saw on the screen, expanding it into the culture at large. However, the 'Third Wave'
of *Rocky* fans, which can be called Generation Y, or more frequently now, Millennials,
depending on where an individual's birthdate falls, have quite a different quandary.

Progeny in the New Millennium
The Millennials, born roughly between the 1980s and 1990s, experienced *Rocky* as
teens beginning in the late 1990s to today. Currently the Gay Rights platform has expanded to include more focused attention on social equality, including gay marriage
and representation in the media. While there are still places hostile to queer youth, the
safe-space community of *Rocky* is now out-and-proud as a political and social ideology. More than just queer sexual rights, full societal inclusion is sought. Ultimately, it is
no longer the dreaming of Baby Boomers or Generation X, it is about actually *being it*.

Thus, the Millennials of the 2000s provide an interesting precipice for *Rocky*. As
the political force and cultural exposure of the LGBTQ community is ever-expanding,
from marriage legislation, to Gay Pride parades that take over cities for days, *Rocky* is
at risk of fading into the background of the floorshow. The remaining live casts, as well

**Doing the Time Warp: Youth Culture,
Coming-of-Age and *The Rocky Horror Picture Show* Through the Years**
Taos Glickman and Shawn DeMille

as the popular Halloween seasonal events, take on an even greater importance in keeping Frank-N-Furter's progeny going along with the social justice imperative of, 'Don't dream it, be it'.

Four decades have passed along with several generations of teens. It is up to the *Rocky* adults of today to pass on the history and importance of Dr Frank-N-Furter's mission. Cleverly hidden in *Rocky Horror*'s various genres and 'camp' dazzle lies a deeper rhetoric of social change, churning throughout the years. It allowed Baby Boomers to see themselves and be themselves, even if just in the dark. It showed Generation X that queer sexuality had a home beyond the fear and ignorance; and now the Millennial teens forge their way.

Frank needs you to put on your fishnets and spread (the word). *The Rocky Horror Picture Show* incorporates the history of the birth of the modern Post-Stonewall Gay Rights first seen by the Baby Boomers in the 1970s. During the 1980s and 1990s, Generation X kept sexual satis...faction bawdy and bold, and today's teens need to take this ideology of queer acceptance and inclusion, and keep giving it a floorshow. In the end, it is up to all of us to see that the Millennials and beyond, don't just dream it, but continue to be it for many generations to come. ●

GO FURTHER

Books

The Classical Hollywood Cinema: Film Style & Mode of Production to 1960
David Bordwell, Janet Staiger and Kristin Thompson
(New York: Columbia University Press, 1985)

Hollywood Genres: Formulas, Filmmaking, and the Studio System
Thomas Schatz
(New York: McGraw-Hill, 1981)

Extracts/Essays/Articles

'Gay Power Circa 1970'
Richard Meyer
In *GLQ: A Journal of Lesbian & Gay Studies*. 12: 3 (2006), pp. 441–64.

'The Function of the Fetish in *The Rocky Horror Picture Show* and *Priscilla, Queen of the Desert*'

31

Betty Robbins and Roger Myrick
In *Journal of Gender Studies*. 9: 3 (2000), pp. 269–80.

'Postmodern Gay Dionysus: Dr. Frank N. Furter'
Amittai F. Aviram
In *Journal of Popular Culture*. 26: 3 (1992), pp. 183–93.

'Semiology Goes to the Midnight Movie'
Bruce McDonald
In *ETC: A Review of General Semantics*. 37: 3 (1980), pp. 216–23.

'The Rocky Horror Picture Show: More Than a Lip Service'
Mark Siegel
In *Science Fiction Studies*. 7: 3 (1980), pp. 305–12.

'Living with Television: The Violence Profile'
George Gerbner and Larry Gross
In *Journal of Communication*. 26 (1976), pp. 172–99.

'Notes on Camp'
Susan Sontag
In *Against Interpretation and Other Essays* (New York: Macmillan, 1966 [1964]), pp. 275-293.

Online

Participation: http://www.rockyhorror.com/participation/

Fan Appreciation no. 2
Shawn Stutler, Director of
Rocky Horror Saved My Life

Interviewed by Marisa C. Hayes

Marisa C. Hayes (MCH): *When did you first get the idea to create the documentary* Rocky Horror Saved My Life? *Describe how it came about and your inspiration behind the film.*

Shawn Stutler (SS): I have thought about producing a documentary on the fans, collectors and live performers that comprise the *Rocky Horror* community since I first became interested in film-making, but I began considering producing this project in earnest during the summer of 2013, after a few of my friends had some success with crowd-funding other creative endeavours. Along with the announcement that the Home of Happiness would be hosting the 40th Anniversary Rocky Horror Convention in 2015, it seemed like we were in the right time, and the right place, to make this dream a reality.

Larry Viezel, executive producer [adds]: There have been several other *Rocky Horror* documentaries over the years. But none of them really were from the fan's perspective. Most of them told our story from the point of view of 'Look at these weirdos who attend this same movie over and over again'. None of them really did anything beyond just one or two markets. And none of them captured why we do it – how it's more than just a movie we are attending. How it's a weekly family gathering. There are lifelong bonds that came about and continue to come about because this film is still playing in theatres.

When the Blu-ray featurette came out it really did a number on the community. It had the potential to really showcase the passion behind the hobby, but what it really did was pit us against each other in an American Idol style of audition process. That's not what we are about, but that's what got filmed.

This documentary is about telling the stories of why *Rocky Horror* is more than just a movie. It's an experience we all both create and celebrate with our family members. An experience that goes on 52 weeks a year in theatres across the globe. It's about a sense of community and a passion we all share and love. *Rocky Horror* is a place where all the misfits from all walks of life get to feel like they belong. And we get to shine doing what we love.

MCH: *Tell us a little about the response you received following the announcement of film production. I know you generated an overwhelming amount of support and interest through your crowd funding campaign on Kickstarter.*

Fan Appreciation no. 2
Shawn Stutler

SS: The response we've received to our *Rocky Horror Saved My Life* campaign has been extremely supportive, and overwhelmingly positive. Not
only do we get the chance to interview people we've known and respected for the last twenty years, we also get to discuss with them our common
passion for *The Rocky Horror Picture Show* and its effect on our lives.

MCH: *What has surprised you the most about your experiences documenting RHPS's influence on audiences? Can you give us an idea of the
different places you have or will be filming?*

SS: What surprised me the most about our experiences documenting
the *Rocky Horror* community is that there is no single formula for success. From Rhode Island to Houston, from Virginia to Washington State,
every show is different, and what works in one city will go over like a lead
balloon in another. What matters is connecting to your audience, and giving them the best show that you can.

MCH: *Can you give us any info on the film's premiere and how it will be
available (online, via DVD, etc.)?*

SS: We plan to premiere *Rocky Horror Saved My Life* at the 40th Anniversary Rocky Horror Convention in New York City next year. After that,
we will have the documentary available on HD Digital Download, Blu-
ray and DVD to fulfil the Rewards and Perks of our crowd-funding campaign. Then, we hope to take the film on the road for exhibition at all the
theatres we used as locations. We'll be pretty busy for the next couple
of years, but I can't think of anything I'd rather do than tour the country
promoting the *Rocky Horror* community, and celebrating the movie that
binds us all together. ●

*For more information, see the film's website: http://www.rockyhorror-
savedmylife.com*

The crew of Rocky Horror Saved My Life meeting Lou Adler, from left to right: Paulie DeLarge, Larry Viezel, Lou Adler, Shawn Stutler and Boo Stewart.

Chapter
03

Shadowing the Boss: Leadership and the Collective Creation of a Frank-N-Furter Identity in Rocky Horror Fan Casts

Tara Chittenden

→ I was fifteen when I muscled my way into mimicking the role of Dr. Frank N. Furter for the Friday night slots at Teaneck's Cedar Lane Theater. I'd seen it a few times at the Waverly and then on Eighth Street and there were always dozens of people who donned fishnets just to be in the audience. Everybody wanted to be Tim Curry. Even Riff Raff.
(Tony Sokol, 'Tim Curry: A Career Retrospective')

Figure 1: Tim Curry's Frank the boss © Twentieth Century Fox.

Dr Frank-N-Furter is arguably the star of *The Rocky Horror Picture Show*. As a leader, Frank is charming, smooth and narcissistic, with an air of arrogance, vanity and at times violence. On-screen, the apparent leader–subordinate relationship between Frank and other characters is set from the start and one of the first references to Frank is from Riff Raff who, answering the door to Brad and Janet, talks of the 'Master'; later explaining that Riff and his sister Magenta 'are but his servants'. Frank's own entrance on-screen shows him march from the elevator, throwing his cape to drape and claim ownership of his throne, and strut to the water cooler turning to reveal a large 'BOSS' tattoo on his upper-right arm (see Figure 1). Frank's status as leader, evident in his throne, tattoo and the sheer attention his arrival commands, is immediately enforced as he passes from the cooler along the meet-and-greet line of convention guests.

This character has a clear magnetism for many fans, yet the opening quote raises an interesting question: are shadow cast members donning the corset to become Frank or are they instead performing Tim Curry? 'Shadowing the Boss' might mean a number of things in the context of this chapter: from exactly mimicking the gestures and timing of Tim Curry on-screen to a position of learning Frank's traits and leadership behaviours to be able to perform them as one's own. Each cast seeks new ways to put their own mark on the show and create a unique cast identity which goes beyond the movie itself. In so doing these fan groups create a collective leadership, which Alexander Haslam describes as:

the creation, co-ordination and control of a shared sense of 'us'. Within this relationship neither the individual nor the group is static. What 'us' means is negotiable, and so too is the contribution that leaders and followers make to any particular definition of 'us-ness'.

Categorization as a member of a fan group can be a significant part of an individual's self-identity and shadow cast members often talk about 'family' and 'community' when describing their group. These fans derive a profound sense of belonging, of 'us-ness', from sharing their fanship with others. Yet, fan studies to date have tended to privilege fan attachment to objects/idols over interactions with other fans and, as such, fail to account

Shadowing the Boss: Leadership and the Collective Creation of a Frank-N-Furter Identity in Rocky Horror Fan Casts
Tara Chittenden

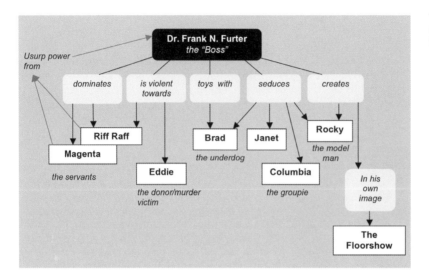

Figure 2: Frank's screen relationships © Tara Chittenden.

for fandom as a site of communal struggles, hierarchies and sense of group identification. Michael Hogg describes social identity theory as:

> a social psychological analysis of the behaviour of people in groups – what happens within groups and between groups […] the fundamental tenet is that the groups we are in define a crucial aspect of who we are, our collective self-concept and our social identity.

Drawing on Hogg's social identity approach to leadership and informal interviews with a number of shadow cast members, I propose Frank-N-Furter as the manifestation of a cast's 'us-ness', questioning how cast Franks understand their performance in relation to Tim Curry's portrayal and how screen Frank's leadership translates to the cast dynamics.

Frank as screen boss
On-screen Frank engages in a variety of relationships with his 'subordinate others' (see Figure 2), dominating every scene he is in and demanding attention from co-characters and audience alike. Frank is 'Master' to servants Riff Raff and Magenta, who ultimately stage a coup to usurp control for themselves. The arrival of Brad and Janet showcase Frank's seductive side (with both Brad and Janet), but also situates Brad as the underdog who attempts to stand up to Frank's dominance. Columbia is portrayed as a 'groupie' who was a 'regular Frankie Fan' but feels used – 'chewed up and spat out' by Frank – disillusioned by his once magnetic charm. There's Rocky, who Frank moulds into his ideal man, and an emergent narcissism which reigns during the floorshow where Frank turns the Medusa-transduced Janet, Brad, Rocky, Columbia and Dr Scott into himself using costume and make-up.

Arguably one of the most interesting dynamics between the characters on-screen is that between Frank and his 'faithful handyman'. Frank exercises a traditional form of leadership with his servant, yet Riff is a subtle character, the employee who's smarter than his boss. In the 'Time Warp', when Riff sings 'I've got to keep control', he knows he should be in charge and considers himself the real leader, foreshadowing the moment in

the floorshow when he and Magenta assume power.

In his lab, Frank claims to have discovered the 'secret to life itself' and his creation, Rocky, is brought to life. During the ensuing celebration, Riff turns the wheel winching Rocky higher and higher into the air and causing Frank to lurch over and kick him away; Frank's violence towards Riff re-emerges later when Riff chases Rocky away with a burning candelabra and Frank whips him for letting Rocky escape.

Yet, Frank, despite his dark periods of tyranny, has an ability to charm. During the floorshow when Riff announces: 'Frank-N-Furter, it's all over. Your mission is a failure, your lifestyle's too extreme. I'm your new commander, you now are my prisoner', Frank's immediate reaction is to try to charm his way out of any punishment: 'Wait. I can explain'. These final scenes for Frank resonate with Robert Price who plays Frank with the Royal Mystic Order of Chaos (Houston, Texas):

'I'm coming home' is an important song for me because it seems to be the glorified goodbye that the oppressed deserve but never get. It expresses hope in the face of adversity, and martyrizes Frank with a sincerity that is unprecedented in such a camp film. The climax when Frank is ultimately killed sticks in my mind because of the line 'society must be protected'. I try my best to portray real fear and disbelief in those moments as I see them as representative of the everyday persecution of the inherently different.

For Price, at the core of Frank is 'a very identifiable want to be loved, which is met with a stark reality of being alone'. He notes that 'all of his manipulation, drug use, seduction and playing God land him face down in a pool, twas beauty that killed the beast', suggesting: 'I am sure he began as a little alien watching American television and movies and hoping one day he could be just like them' (and this speculation may go some way to describe the types of leadership role Frank assumes: God, Scientist, Tyrant, Heroine, Casanova). Liz Locke describes how Frank succeeds in winning our hearts:

to such an extent that, even when he whips his faithful handyman until he cries for mercy, abuses Janet, shoves Brad to the ground, and kills Eddie, the audience and his on-screen groupies not only forgive him, but emulate him.

**Shadowing the Boss: Leadership and the Collective Creation
of a Frank-N-Furter Identity in Rocky Horror Fan Casts**
Tara Chittenden

Shadowing the boss

Men/women mid 20s to 45 years of age in good physical shape. An engaging flamboyant personality that can cross the threshold between genders and be comfortable doing it. A team player with charisma both on and off the stage. A quick mind with a quick
wit. Of course a dancer and skilled at make-up. Must be willing to create their own
Frank outside of the Tim Curry prototype. A rock star. Able to walk in high heels a must.
(The Royal Mystic Order of Chaos)

Above is just one example of a casting call for Frank. It calls for charisma and the ability
to perform in heels, but makes explicit the need to go beyond Tim Curry's 'prototype' –
perhaps informed by the cast leader's experience of seeing the *Rocky Horror* stage show:

The characters were recognizable but they didn't wear the movie costumes. I think
that encouraged [us] to take our characters and costumes beyond the movie… While
I enjoy shows that can exactly mimic the movie, I much prefer shows where the performers take a risk with their characters. (Jeff Foss, The Royal Mystic Order of Chaos)

Robert Price, Chaos's Frank, addresses the 'Tim or Frank?' question: 'Richard O'Brien
wrote Frank N. Furter, but Tim Curry made him dynamic. Studying the film moment to moment you get a sense of how clear and intense every action and tactic are for Frank'. The
goal of most cast Franks is not just to create a Tim Curry lookalike, but also to craft their
own identity through the costume – to perform Frank as a mix of O'Brien's text creation,
Curry's interpretation and the cast's extension of both. Price hopes that his own performance 'is taking Tim Curry's characterization and letting it explode into a million different
shades of perspective'.
Whilst casts range from those who aim for perfect body and lip-synced screen accu-
racy to those who take a more ad-libbed approach, Deme Trachy from Formal Dress Optional (Newark, Delaware) explains the need to privilege Curry's version:

Most shadow cast Franks, including myself, focus more on embodying the version of
Frank N. Furter played by Tim Curry, rather than the original Frank from the Rocky Horror Show. Mostly because that is the version that the audiences who come to watch
our show see on the screen. The majority of the audiences who come to our shows
have never seen the Rocky Horror Show […] throwing other references at them would
be confusing.

The 'shadow' of the cast was initially about simultaneity, about demonstrating fanship,
that one has seen the film so often as to have the timing and gestures down pat. But the
activities of shadow casts have extended far beyond pure synchrony and include any

number of 'theme nights' – for example 'Zombies', 'Buffy the Vampire Slayer', 'The Simpsons' – where the cast blend other screen references with their *Rocky* characters. So, in 'The Simpsons' night, Frank takes on a yellow hue and Homer joins Tim Curry and O'Brien's Frank in a complex cultural blender of characterization. Cast Franks are caught between two goals: on one hand to become a perfect shadow to Tim Curry's Frank, but on the other to make the role their own in a way which distinguishes it from the screen performance – yet not to the extent of audience alienation. Marilyn Brewer's optimal distinctiveness theory posits that people must balance the need for inclusiveness and belongingness with the need for distinctiveness. So whilst Franks are embedded in the style of their cast, individuals do still seek recognition and reputation for their work amongst the wider *Rocky* fan community.

One prime difference between screen and shadow cast is that the film is edited and cut through close-ups and multiple camera angles which determine what the viewer sees at any one time and what is hidden outside the frame. Screen Frank disappears when the camera is pointed elsewhere; shadow Frank cannot. Though at times this form of *Rocky Horror* fanship might feel more about the relationship with a screen image (with shape and timing) than the character of Frank himself, an ability to become *as* Frank for off-screen moments means that playing this role is as much about wearing the personality traits of the character as it is wearing the costume; as Chaos's Robert Price explains: 'the character is in command in the film, and yet is playful, melodramatic, frightening and over all manipulative. When I play Frank I try to be all of those things, but turned up to eleven so the back row can feel it'. Embodying the character, physically and mentally, can provide a form of escapism for the individual, whilst the cast context retains a strong feeling of support; Deme Trachy describes:

> the second the stage lights hit me, I am no longer ME, but whichever character I am playing that night. And everything that I do from the moment the lights come on, to the moment I step out for curtain call, IS that character. In this way, Rocky Horror has helped me on a personal level, due to its ability to make me forget about whatever problems I am having in life, and focus on the performance. (Formal Dress Optional)

Frenchy Lunning identifies a 'transversal moment': a 'display of multiple identity eruptions [that] begins precisely as the costume is put on'. For Lunning, such transversal moments 'seem to create this potential space of creativity and collectivity'. In this moment, a shadow cast's Frank is not purely a fan's emulation of Tim Curry, rather s/he is a manifestation of the cast processes of, in H. Peter Dachler and Dian-Marie Hosking's words:

Shadowing the Boss: Leadership and the Collective Creation of a Frank-N-Furter Identity in Rocky Horror Fan Casts
Tara Chittenden

Figure 5: Robert Price as
Frank © The Royal Mystic
Order of Chaos/Robert Pric

'interaction, conversation, narrating, dialoguing, and multiloguing', which together bring a three-dimensionality to the shadow form.

The collective creation of a Frank identity

Each shadow cast has its own personality; consequently, 'social identity' for cast members becomes what it means to be 'us' in the context of not only US-based, but international, shadow casts. Because, as Hogg describes, 'people cognitively represent social groups in terms of prototypes – a "fuzzy set" of attributes, such as people's attitudes and behaviours, which defines and evaluates one category and distinguishes it from other categories'; this may locate Frank-N-Furter as the prototype character through which others fans 'judge' the quality or personality of each cast. Prototypes capture similarities within a group as well as differences between that group and other groups; thus, casts perceive others through the lens of in-group and out-group prototypes ('*our* Frank is like...'; '*their* Frank is like...') rather than actors as unique individuals. The implication is that if leadership is produced by these social-psychological processes, then for an individual to be effective as a leader in a shadow cast (rather than the titular 'cast leader') s/he must display the prototypical or normative characteristics of an in-group member for that cast.

Cast members who are highly prototypical (or 'very Tim Curry'), may by definition embody central and desirable aspects of the cast group more so than other members. In those casts which aim for perfect lip and body synchrony, prototypical members – those who conform most closely to their screen counterpart – can appear as the standard for other members, and thus appear to be the source of influence over the group. Whereas screen Frank exercises a vertical leadership that entails the process of one individual assuming dominance over others, social identity leadership entails the process of shared influence between and among individuals. Within this perspective appointed cast leaders/directors share responsibility with others for the construction of a particular understanding of the character relationships and their enactment. Tor Johnson, cast director of Interchangeable Parts (Seminole, Florida), explains:

> Being Director is not about lording over them, but listening to them, helping improve the ideas they have, we look at ourselves as a family, we work together, not as a kingdom where one rules above all, even as Director I have to follow the rules we all agreed upon.

For Chaos's Robert Price:

> how Frank treats the show influences the rest of the cast greatly. I think it would be easy to fall into playing as an individual rather than working off each other, especially as Frank. The important thing for me is not to be a Boss to the cast (cause I'm not in charge anyway) but to play with them as a team.

Members who have performed with different casts acknowledge the need to adapt their performance to the 'rules' of whichever cast they are in at the time; Interchangeable Parts' Tor Johnson describes:

> While I think my Riff is a great way to perform, it is also the [Interchangeable Parts] version of Riff, if I went and performed for another cast […] I would ask them how they wanted me to act, it is not Ip's show… I would be very rude if I didn't perform to how the rules were for another cast and expected them to accept me doing my own thing.

So, a performance perfectly synced to the screen does not necessarily mean one perfectly synced to the cast and for this reason Frank cannot be an isolated leader. A character is not conceptualized around an individual's interpretation and performance, but a collective cast construction and one that varies amongst the different 'families'. Beyond this, Johnson's comment reveals that the characterization resides with the cast – as a fundamental part of its 'us-ness' – and is not carried with the individual actor between casts. Kenneth Murrell describes leadership as shared responsibility: 'a social act, a construction of a "ship" as a collective vehicle to help take us where we as a group, organization or society desire to go'. Here, shadow casts are not only collectively constructing each character, but in so doing, are also constructing a fanship.

Conclusion

For shadow casts there is a shift from Frank as boss-*in*-relationships with other screen characters to Frank-*as*-the relationship and a manifestation of the 'us-ness' of the cast. This fanship is not just about collecting memorabilia and/or producing content for fansites, but becoming – inhabiting – the very core of the character. A social identity

Shadowing the Boss: Leadership and the Collective Creation
of a Frank-N-Furter Identity in Rocky Horror Fan Casts
Tara Chittenden

theory of leadership includes the study of group interactions and the social dynamics and constructions of leadership which emerge from interpersonal relationships. By studying leadership as it occurs relationally within fan collectives, researchers have an opportunity to account for many more of the social forces working to influence fan behaviours.

Benyamin Lichtenstein, Mary Uhl-Bien and their co-authors define a 'leadership event' as 'a perceived segment of action whose meaning is created by the interactions of actors involved in producing it'. Here, the Frank role is the perceived segment of action and its meaning created by the interactions of cast members involved in shaping the character. Bill Henkin states that 'most fans feel that it is preferable for responses to grow organically from the local culture' – thus casts introduce character gestures and call backs (segments of action) which are topical and relate to something meaningful to the local audience, further enhancing the cast's own identity.

An important aspect of the shadow cast's identity is the construction and dynamics of the fan group, including inner tensions and struggles over roles, but also the support which goes along with belonging to such a group. We often derive self-esteem from our group memberships and fan affiliations, and by aligning themselves with their cast and the wider *Rocky Horror* community, fans are able to feel a part of something special which serves to validate their self-worth and sense of belonging:

> Just as in any social group, there can be quite a bit of drama and gossip in a shadow cast... Each issue that arises, though, for the most part is talked about and worked out. Being part of a Rocky Horror shadowcast is like being part of a large family, who happens to like to run around in their underwear in front of an audience of people. (Deme Trachy, Formal Dress Optional)

Moments of disagreement and creative collision can be what pushes a cast to take the show into truly innovative and provocative directions. After all, a bit of friction is good. But, as the boss said: 'I don't want no dissension. Just dynamic tension'. ●

~~~~~~~~~~~~

GO FURTHER

Books

Psychology in Organizations: The Social Identity Approach
Alexander Haslam
(London: Sage, 2001)

The Rocky Horror Picture Show Book
Bill Henkin
(New York: Hawthorn Books, 1979)

Essays/Extracts/Articles

'Cosplay, Drag, and the Performance of Abjection'
Frenchy Lunning

In Timothy Perper and Martha Cornog (eds). *Mangatopia: Essays on Manga and Anime in the Modern World* (Santa Barbara, CA: Libraries Unlimited, 2011), pp. 71–89.

'Complexity Leadership Theory: An Interactive Perspective on Leading in Complex Adaptive Systems'

Benyamin Lichtenstein, Mary Uhl-Bien, Ross Marion, Anson Seers, James Douglas Orton and Craig Schreiber
In *Emergence: Complexity and Organization*. 8: 4 (2006), pp. 2–12.

'One of Us: Social Identity, Group Belonging and Leadership'
Michael Hogg

In B. Kellerman (ed.). *Center for Public Leadership working papers* (Cambridge, MA: John F. Kennedy School of Government, Harvard University, 2005), Vol. 3, pp. 3–21.

'Optimal Distinctiveness, Social Identity and the Self'
Marilyn Brewer
In Mark R. Leary and June P. Tangney (eds). *Handbook of Self and Identity* (New York: Guildford, 2003), pp. 480–91.

'Social Categorization, Depersonalization, and Group Behavior'
Michael Hogg

**Shadowing the Boss: Leadership and the Collective Creation
of a Frank-N-Furter Identity in Rocky Horror Fan Casts**
Tara Chittenden

In Michael Hogg and Scott Tindale (eds). *Blackwell Handbook of Social Psychology: Group Processes* (Oxford: Blackwell, 2001), pp. 56–85.

'Don't Dream It, Be It: The Rocky Horror Picture Show as Cultural Performance'
Liz Locke
In *New Directions in Folklore*. 3 (1999) [Online], https://scholarworks.iu.edu/dspace/bit-stream/handle/2022/7209/NDiF_issue_3_article_2.pdf?sequence=1.

'Emergent Theories of Leadership for the Next Century: Towards Relational Concepts'
Kenneth Murrell
In *Organization Development Journal*. 15: 3 (1997), pp. 35–42.

'The Primacy of Relations in Socially Constructing Organizational Realities'
H. Peter Dachler and Dian-Marie Hosking
In Dian-Marie Hosking, H. Peter Dachler and Kenneth Gergen (eds). *Management and Organization: Relational Alternatives to Individualism* (Aldershot: Averbury, 1995), pp. 1–29.

Online

'Tim Curry: A Career Retrospective'
Tony Sokol
Den of Geek. 3 February 2013, http://www.denofgeek.us/movies/55873/tim-curry-a-career-retrospective.

The Royal Mystic Order of Chaos: www.rockyhorrorhouston.com

Formal Dress Optional: www.formaldressoptional.org

Interchangeable Parts: www.rhpsip.com

'THERE'S NO CRIME IN GIVING YOURSELF OVER TO PLEASURE.'

FRANK-N-FURTER

Chapter
04

'A Strange Journey': Finding Carnival in *The Rocky Horror Picture Show*

Molly McCourt

→ It will be a sad day when a too smart audience will read *Casablanca* as conceived by Michael Curtiz after reading Calvino and Barthes. But that day will come.
(Umberto Eco, 'Casablanca: Cult Movies and Intertextual Collage')

Introduction

Eco writes these words in the conclusion of his essay in which he argues that cult movies are mostly meant for purposes of entertainment and not analysis. In kind, one may use the same critique of this venture. Does merit exist in interpreting *The Rocky Horror Picture Show* as directed by Jim Sharman after having read Francois Rabelais and Mikhail Bakhtin? I would like to argue that the spirit of these three entities would not allow this experience to 'be a sad day'. In fact, uncovering the ways in which a sixteenth-century French author's ideas live on in both Russian literary criticism and Anglo-American popular culture of the twentieth century reveals that the roots of *RHPS* run quite deep. The text's already rich history as a British stage show, Anglo-American motion picture and global cult phenomenon in the twentieth century actually reaches back to scandalous Renaissance literature half a millennia prior to the first ever performance of the 'Time Warp'.

To begin, we must first identify what Mikhail Bakhtin really means when he writes about 'carnival' – the word that is to be ubiquitous in this essay. In the sixteenth century, Francois Rabelais focused his stories of feasting and debauchery on this concept, which – as described by Bakhtin in *Rabelais and His World* (1984) – 'celebrated a temporary liberation from the prevailing truth and from the established order; it marked the suspension of all hierarchical rank, privileges, norms, and prohibitions'. The constant throughout all tenets of this alternate reality is the idea of a 'world upside-down'. Bakhtin rediscovered Rabelais's fiction in the 1940s and expanded upon the carnivalesque themes of death and rebirth, crowning of a clownish king, marriage of the sacred and the profane and festival as a second life in *Rabelais and His World*. This essay adds yet another layer of exploration with a Transylvanian text, arguing that Bakhtin's interpretation of 'carnival' flows throughout much more of the 'Late Night Double Feature' than previous research posits. Without further ado, in the words of *RHPS*'s criminologist: 'I would like, if I may, to take you on a strange journey'.

Death and rebirth

To begin examining the many layers of text involved in this undertaking, Liz Locke's essay on the cultural performance of *RHPS* refers to the many generic allusions as the 'cannibalistically intertextual extreme'. Locke is referring to the patchwork of elements from horror, science fiction, Gothic romances and biker films that *RHPS* possesses to create a work of cinema unlike any of its predecessors. '*RHPS* swallows everything its makers could lay their cognition on', Locke explains, listing the many genres and styles of film from which this 'Late Night Double Feature' borrows. In short, the work both consumes and gives birth simultaneously, nodding toward Bakhtin's grotesque tenet of carnival: death and rebirth. This concept first takes shape in the very beginning of the film as the midnight showing audience calls out in the dark: 'And in the beginning, God said "Let there be lips!" And there were lips and they were good'. In the opening

'A Strange Journey':
Finding Carnival in The Rocky Horror Picture Show
Molly McCourt

credits, bright red lips appear out of the black void of the screen and begin singing to the audience. The image of the mouth is important when considering the original plan for this introductory sequence. In Locke's essay, she writes: 'Originally, the initial sequence was scripted not with lips, but a montage of scenes from the ten classic science fiction films mentioned in the opening song'. Rather than visually feature these sci-fi films, it's as if the mouth has already swallowed them, only to give birth to this new kind of cinematic event. While Richard Sharman, director of *RHPS*, could have chosen other ways to start the movie, he unknowingly fulfils Bakhtin's image of the mouth floating in an abyss.

After the lips disappear at the end of the opening credits, the story of Brad and Janet begins as they attend the wedding and promptly get engaged. Because the happy couple sings a lively song to accompany this joyous moment, they seem completely unaware that they are dancing around the tombstones of a cemetery. Birth and death are again paired; the proposal as the birth of impending married life and literal death as evidenced in tombstones and funeral preparations. Locke points to yet another pairing of death and birth by connecting the coffin and Rocky's birth vat, citing Riff Raff, Magenta and Columbia's appearance first as pallbearers and later as laboratory assistants during Rocky's creation as witnesses to both the end and beginning of life.

Figure 1: 'Let there be lips!' floating in an abyss © Twentieth Century Fox.

Figure 2: The uncrowning of the Rabelasian king © Twentieth Century Fox.

Rabelais's king

Turning to the man who 'holds the secret to life itself' leads to an exploration of Dr Frank-N-Furter as a Rabelaisian king. Turning again to *Rabelais and His World*, Bakhtin begins describing the popular festive image of a king in Rabelais's fiction as 'abused and beaten when the time of his reign is over', which is quite evident in the mutiny that his servants, Riff Raff and Magenta, stage against Frank. Desperate to return to Transylvania, the siblings forcibly end Frank's rule over the castle by threat of a laser beam of pure antimatter. Bakhtin goes on to write: 'Abuse reveals the other, true face of the abused; it tears off his disguise and mask. It is the king's uncrowning'. As a response to the death threat, Frank attempts to explain himself in a sentimental solo entitled, 'I'm Going Home'. While singing, he removes his disguise, by dramatically wiping away his blue eye shadow and red lipstick. In doing so, Frank surrenders the feminine identity he has so carefully constructed. No longer the sexy scientist Frank stands merely as a frightened, uncertain man dressed in woman's lingerie.

After the uncrowning, ultimately death comes to this king. After Frank is struck with

Riff Raff's beam of antimatter, Rocky carries Frank up the RKO Radio Tower, re-enacting the wrath of King Kong as he rescued Faye Ray. As Rocky reaches the top, he loses strength from repeated laser blows, and both the king and his creation fall dead into the pool of 'warm waters of sins of the flesh' (Sharman). As Bakhtin references earlier, 'in this system, death is followed by regeneration'. Fortuitously, the film's parting shot – Riff Raff and Magenta 'doing the Time Warp again' – creates the idea of carnival's unending cycle. Locke nods to this death and renewal of story through the king's fate, claiming 'if there is no crucifixion, there can be no resurrection'. Referencing the Book of Timothy in the St James Bible, comparing Frank to Christ, the 'King of kings', further suggests his place as the Rabelaisian king of a world turned inside out.

The union of the sacred and the profane in *RHPS*

In Bakhtin's *The Dialogic Imagination* (first published as a whole in 1975), he claims carnival has the power to 'bring together that which has been traditionally kept distant and disunified'. With this in mind, *RHPS* successfully celebrates Rabelaisian carnival by combining the sacred and the profane, oftentimes creating an inverse relationship

Figure 3: The sweet transvestite 'draped blasphemously pieta-like over a throne'
© Twentieth Century Fox.

Figure 4: Michelangelo's Pietà (1498) © ObviousMag.org.

between the two. I will examine three specific scenes saturated with the inversion of the sacred and the profane, which also allude to Frank as a Christly figure. The first scene reveals Frank both as the master of the house and the resident sex symbol. After Brad and Janet witness the 'folk-dancing' routine of the 'Time Warp' the elevator descends, producing Frank-N-Furter in pearls and six-inch platform heels, stomping to the beat of his opening song, 'Sweet Transvestite'. While he informs his new guests of the recent events of his castle, his servants gather around him, kneeling with simultaneous reverence and fanaticism. Locke refers to Frank's presiding over the Annual Transylvanian Convention as one 'draped blasphemously pieta-like over a throne'. Here, Frank becomes conflated with the famous image of the crucified 'King of Kings' and as fellow Transylvanians, his disciples are equally profane.

Further, as Frank invites Brad and Janet to 'stay for the night/or maybe a bite', Columbia makes an obscene gesture toward Frank's bare leg, devilishly biting down, then licking her lips. Extending the metaphor of Frank as a Christ figure, a 'bite' of Frank denotes a twisted Eucharist. Bakhtin supports this possibility with his description of Rabelais's interpretation of Christ's final words. According to Bakhtin, in Rabelais's novel, 'Christ's last words on the cross, *sitio* ('I thirst') and *consummatum est* ('it is consum-

'A Strange Journey':
Finding Carnival in The Rocky Horror Picture Show
Molly McCourt

mated') are travestied into terms of eating and overindulgence'. Indeed, considering the sexual acts that Frank performs on Brad and Janet as well as the orgiastic festivities, eating and indulging occur repeatedly.

As the night in Frank's castle progresses, *RHPS* re-enacts their own version of the Last Supper scene. The criminologist introduces this idea, calling it 'the breaking of the bread, the last meal of the condemned man, and now, this meal'. Frank's distribution of food and toast ('To absent friends') mirrors Jesus' offering of bread and his request to his disciples in Luke's Gospel to drink 'in remembrance of me'. Furthermore, the staging of the meal itself supplies a barrage of profane imagery. Multiple characters are wearing lingerie at a formal dining-room table that blends crystal drinking glasses with plastic cups. Magenta and Riff Raff serve wine; however, the servants spill it, illustrating their own indifference. The dinner guests are startled by the sound of Frank's electric carving knife amidst silver serving platters. Lastly, in a final profane gesture, Frank reaches for a plastic ketchup bottle as he begins to feast. This image is a far cry from DaVinci's *Last Supper* painting (1495-1498), yet the criminologist's allusion to the biblical image makes known that the film intends to challenge the sacred, while the details of the scene prove the mischievous nature of this confrontation.

After dinner, Frank jumps into 'warm waters of sins of the flesh', unifying the sacred and profane once more by lounging in a life preserver with the words 'S.S. Titanic' emblazoned on the side. This troubling combination brings with it both the urging to experience sinful sexuality and the desecration of tragedy. Not only is Frank encouraging surrender to 'absolute pleasure', but he is also abusing the function of his buoy. Frank almost seems to be flaunting the life-saving power of his own quest for pleasure in the face of massive loss of life in the *Titanic*'s sinking. Also, as the fog clears, the entire floor to the pool reveals a replication of Michelangelo's *The Creation of Adam* (circa 1511). Clearly implying that these 'warm waters' are life giving, this is a true conflation of the sacred and the profane. For both God and Adam to see, the half-clothed characters of Brad, Janet, Rocky and Columbia join Frank in the pool for a beautifully messy sexual free-for-all. Finally, considering the original location of *The Awakening of Adam* – the ceiling of the Sistine Chapel – this pool represents both an ultimate profaning of the scared, but also – quite literally – a striking illustration of Bakhtin's 'world upside down'.

The union of the sacred and profane in the *RHPS* experience

As many readers are certainly familiar, the *RHPS* experience requires the chaotic harmony of three elements: the rolling film, the living actors performing the film, and the audience who verbally and kinaesthetically respond to the film/performance. Patrick Kinkade and Michael Katovich expand upon this cult audience in their essay 'Toward a Sociology of Cult Films: Reading "Rocky Horror"' (1992). Kinkade and Katovich write: 'Cult filmgoers' paradoxical perspective holds "nothing is sacred," on one hand, and "our film is sacred" on the other'. This 'nothing is sacred' idea is well proven in many of the audience's call outs, while the sacred nature of the film itself is easily recognized by the regularity of viewings and performances. Many attend midnight showings similar to how devout Christians attend Mass, as Locke claims in her cultural study of *RHPS*: 'It's not for everybody, but some hardcore fans call it "going to church"'. This act of communion is characterized in a carnivalesque manner as Kinkade and Katovich emphasize: 'Every midnight across the country, the profane becomes re-elevated into an idiocultural sense of the sacred'. The reoccurrence of the event is just as important to ritual as the repetition of language. Similar to the ways in which religious prayers and responses can change depending on which area of the world is celebrating, so too do the call out scripts of *RHPS*. Although the Cleveland 'liturgy' differs slightly from that of New York's, the shared mission of each show is expressed at the same time with a common lexicon every weekend.

In addition to timing and language, space is also crucial to ritual. While liturgies take place in a church or temple, *RHPS* midnight showings all occur in a movie theatre. As Robert Stam highlights in *Subversive Pleasures* (1989), the components of the 'space of the sacred' and 'time in parentheses' are integral to the sacred and profane in Bakhtin's carnival. Outside of a midnight showing, the movie theatre can be a sacred place that patrons keep tidy and they refrain from distracting conversation during movies. This is how most patrons show their respect for the space. However, as Stam claims, to treat *RHPS* with reverence requires 'a rejection of social decorum entailing a release from oppressive etiquette, politeness, and good manners'. Under this tenet of carnival, one honours the *RHPS* experience by yelling obscene comments, dancing in provocative ways, and throwing toast at the screen. This desecration of the holiness of the movie theatre represents the spatial inversion of the sacred and the profane.

Second life in *RHPS*

Though themes of death, birth, crowning and desecration seem serious, *RHPS* is still meant to be a humorous film. Through watching and experiencing *RHPS*, viewers, actors and audience members are all part of the carnival that Bakhtin calls 'the people's second life, organized around the basis of laughter'. As is the case with much of Rabelais's writing, as well as Bakhtin's criticism of Rabelais's world, gaiety is the main thrust of this prominent idea of carnival.

Stam expands upon this alternate reality, which he refers to as 'a foregrounding of social overturning and the counter hegemonic subversion of established power via "world upside down"'. Regarding the film alone, Brad and Janet's second life exists in the 'night out that they would remember for a very long time' and Bakhtinian carnival simply permeates every room of Frank-N-Furter's castle. Though Brad and Janet are at first resistant to the advances of the denizens of the castle, they eventually surrender their prudence to the hypnotizing power of the 'sins of the flesh'. This wearing down of the virginal couple does not take long, seeing that all Frank has to do is disguise his voice,

'A Strange Journey':
Finding Carnival in The Rocky Horror Picture Show
Molly McCourt

·

play the role of significant other, and argue logically with each person. Frank's simple defence to both characters' concern with infidelity is: 'But it isn't all bad. In fact, I think you'll find it quite pleasurable'. When neither Janet nor Brad can debase Frank's argument, we observe what Kinkade and Katovich claim; 'with these corruption rituals, Brad and Janet quickly shed their innocence'. Frank's liberation of Brad and Janet remains true to this alternate reality – 'the notion of bisexuality and the practice of transvestitism as a release form the burden of socially imposed sex roles' – that Stam claims as one of the key components to Bakhtin's carnival. By giving themselves over to absolute pleasure, Brad and Janet completely abandon their once well-washed Midwest life for the second life of the carnival produced by 'Frank's crazed imagination'.

Although their stay at the Frankenstein place awakens a completely new sexual appetite in Brad and Janet, this journey into a second life is always temporary. Kinkade and Katovich remind us of this as the destruction of Frank-N-Furter's castle and probable nuptials of Brad and Janet 'reaffirm the necessity of a heterosexual procreating society'. This 'mental mind fuck', as Frank calls it, though thrilling, is not meant to replace one's primary life and responsibilities. In kind, Bakhtin writes of a certain explanation of a feast of fools in the sixteenth century in Rabelais's world. Its defenders argue:

> Such gay diversion is necessary so that foolishness, which is our second nature and seems to be inherent in man might freely spend itself at least once a year. Wine barrels burst if from time to time we do not open them and let in some air. We must give it air in order not to let it spoil.

Bakhtin goes on to describe the feast as 'a vent for the second nature of man'. Using this idea of release elevates *RHPS* to its completed form – the cult experience.

Second life in the experience of *RHPS*

True display of 'second life' is revealed in the active participation involved in the midnight showing. Stam's characterization of carnival – 'a liberating explosion of otherness' which 'erases the boundaries between spectator and performer' – is quite fitting in this sense. Whether an individual identifies with the cast, audience or virgins makes no difference, as everyone plays an integral part. Live actors reject the authority of the movie screen behind them, audience members call out in unison or independently, and virgins join in the contagious the 'Time Warp' dance ritual. Costumes, voices, movements and red 'V''s are on display for all to see, hear and share. 'By the light of the night', everyone shares in a collective release of the profane.

And once the criminologist's globe has stopped spinning and the credits roll, as Locke writes: 'most of the participants will re-enter their ordinary contexts and assume their conventional roles as high school students, librarians, shopkeepers, accountants, and countless other mundane professions'. Locke's point not only mirrors the temporary na-

Figure 5: Some midnight showings venture out of the movie house and into dive bars like Timothy's Pub in Dayton, Ohio. Performers and audience members share the same intimate space © Dayton's Annual Transylvania Convention.

ture of carnival, but also demonstrates how the element of audience participation goes beyond what Stam calls 'theatre without the footlights' and also supplies the audience with an opportunity for a kind of second life on an emotional level. Cast members' testimonials showcase the communal escape into a 'world upside down', writing of the hundreds of miles they travel in order to perform in *RHPS* on a weekly basis. Others win roles by reputation that spans across states. According to Locke, a fan favourite is the Navy corporal who gets 'an absolute rush every time he exposes his corseted body' in the role of Frank; all individuals attest to the liberation that a midnight showing offers. Some even choose certain roles over others in order to fulfil a part of themselves in which they never felt truly confident. This temporary authority mirrors the crowning of the unlikely king during a feast of fools in Rabelais's world. *Time* magazine's Richard Corliss even chose to conclude his article on *RHPS* with a quote from a Citibank computer operator who plays Brad in New York's *RHPS* production. He attests:

> At school, I was a nerd, a dork, a social outcast. So of course, I identified with Brad. Now, I'm still a dork, but it's OK. *Rocky Horror* says, 'You're weird, but you belong somewhere. Let's all be weird together!'

Similar feelings of emotional connection and escape surface in an interview Locke held with a man who plays the role of Eddie every weekend. He divulges: 'I work. I pay my bills. But Eddie... he's just like the opposite of all of that. Totally free. When I'm in here, I'm Eddie totally. All the frustrations of the week all go out the door'.

Revellers and carnival kings did not waste moments of the party worrying about their eventual return to everyday life; midnight showing participants follow in these joyful footsteps.

Conclusion

While the projected film, live acting and audience response occur simultaneously, all work to create a cohesive experience. A feeling of unity forms through this phenomenon – an idea that Bakhtin identifies as the life force of carnival during the Renaissance. This was a time that he claims was 'the zenith of carnival life' in *The Problems of Doestoevsky's Poetics* (1984). Once the carnival attitude lost its 'nature of belonging to the whole people', the second life of Rabelais's world faded into the past. *RHPS* will not go that gently. Considering the strong sense of community surrounding the text, as well as its abundant examples of true carnival spirit, this cult film/performance/experience exists not only as an authentic, surviving 'vent' for the mundane routine of the everyday, but an icon of carnival for decades to come. And of those Rockyphiles who 'swim the warm waters of sins of the flesh', I dare say that both Francois Rabelais and Mikhail Bakhtin would be quite proud. ●

'A Strange Journey':
Finding Carnival in The Rocky Horror Picture Show
Molly McCourt

~~~~~~~~~~~~

GO FURTHER

Books

Subversive Pleasures
Robert Stam
(Baltimore/London: Johns Hopkins University Press, 1989)

Rabelais and His World
Mikhail Bakhtin
(Bloomington: Indiana University Press, 1984)

The Problems of Doestoevsky's Poetics
Mikhail Bakhtin
(Minneapolis: University of Minnesota Press, 1984)

The Dialogic Imagination
Mikhail Bakhtin
(Austin: University of Texas Press, 1981)

Extracts/Essays/Articles

'Don't Dream It, Be It: *The Rocky Horror Picture Show* as cultural performance'
Liz Locke
In *New Directions in Folklore*. 3 (1999) [Online], https://scholarworks.iu.edu/dspace/
bitstream/handle/2022/7209/NDiF_issue_3_article_2.pdf?sequence=1.

'Toward a Sociology of Cult Films: Reading "Rocky Horror"'
Patrick T. Kinkade and Michael A. Katovich
In *The Sociological Quarterly*. 33 (1992), pp. 191–208

'Casablanca: Cult Movies and the Intertextual Collage'
Umberto Eco
In David Lodge and Nigel Wood (eds). *Modern Criticism and Theory: A Reader*, 3rd edn
(Edinburgh: Pearson Ed Press, 1988), pp. 462–71.

Online

'Across the Land: The Voice of Rocky Horror'
Richard Corliss
Time.com. 21 June 2005, http://www.time.com/time/magazine/article/0,9171,1074833,00.html.

'WE'VE GOT TO GET OUT OF THIS TRAP! BEFORE THIS... DECADENCE... SAPS OUR WILLS.'

DR EVERETT SCOTT

Fan Appreciation no. 3
Stephanie Freeman, Founder, TimeWarp

Interviewed by Marisa C. Hayes

Marisa C. Hayes (MCH): *TimeWarp organizes an annual picnic weekend at Frank's castle (Oakley Court) and sounds like an amazing alternative to conventions. I imagine it brings together a great crowd of fans from different generations and locations, any special memories or fun anecdotes you can share about the picnic show weekend? And any special insights about the castle you care to tell us about?*

Stephanie Freeman (SF): I approached Oakley Court in 2006 with a view to celebrating TimeWarp's 18th Anniversary, with a costumed picnic idea. It was something we can do in the UK that no one else in the world can take – we have Oakley Court after all! It has steadily grown from its first bash to quite a soirée. We love the fact that the staff enjoy it as much as we do, and that they are happy to fly our own Transylvanian flag as the weekend approaches. There is nothing to quite match that feeling, seeing the flag in the breeze as you drive up to the door of the house. And then to see the film, and be inside the house you are watching on the screen, from the outside, is quite mind bending. There have been a couple of years of picnics where, when the film has finished, we have retired to the terrace with a celebratory drink, and been viewers to a fantastic thunder-and-lightning storm – the perfect end to a *Rocky Horror* Fans' picnic!

MCH: *TimeWarp has been going strong under your leadership (and with Richard O'Brien's blessing) since 1988. How has RHPS fandom evolved since you began? Obviously, there are a lot more resources in easy reach via the Internet now, but do you feel that RHPS fandom in the UK has grown, gone through various periods or remained steady? Compared to the States do you feel there are any key differences in how RHPS fandom has developed in the UK?*

SF: Fandom generally changes every few years – and *Rocky Horror* is no exception. However, the passionate ones are either diehard and have been with it twenty years or more, or there are the new fans who come in with that same passion and burn out after three or four years. Once a stage show tour comes to an end, that is when the diehards are made… and the visiting fans drift to another part of the performing world. Some get so intense they want everything here and now at any cost, and then the flame isn't fanned when the show is off the road, they sell the lot. Been there, done that, and moved on. It is a bit like Marmite, you either love it or hate it. Very few people can take it or leave it and be indifferent as, if it touches you, it usually touches your soul. The Internet changed

Fan Appreciation no. 3
Stephanie Freeman

all fandom irrevocably; the UK has always been a far more free and easy fandom as we are lucky that we don't get very many of the fans who will stop at nothing to meet their favourite actor/see the house/get to a stage show audition… In the USA it is very much film based, whereas in the UK we have the pleasure of both – and we can enjoy it instead of become fixated and compulsive with it. I like that, and I embrace the freedoms we still have over here with *Rocky Horror* compared to elsewhere.

MCH: *Can you explain the 'Singalonga' controversy in the UK to our international readers who might not be familiar with this kind of event? What's your take on it?*

SF: There is no controversy as such – it is just that the *Rocky Horror* film and show have had audience participation LONG before 'Singalonga' came to life. They adopted us, and have taken it on as 'theirs'. But, if it brings new people to see a film screening with a shadow cast or the 'proper' fan-originated audience participation, or to see a live show on tour; suddenly they get it, and they want more of the genuine *Rocky Horror*. Personally, I prefer them, to 'Singalonga'.

MCH: *What's next for TimeWarp? Any special plans or activities you care to share with our readers?*

SF: We celebrated 25 years in 2013, and we are to celebrate our tenth Picnic in 2015. As long as we can spread the word, and keep fans amused, and entertained in between the times when a live stage show is touring, or film screenings happening, then we do what we intended. The best thing to do is stay in touch with the website *www.timewarp.org.uk* and that will tell people what and when and where… and any specials we normally get the scoop on ahead of the general release info… so all is good. ●

For more information, contact: www.timewarp.org.uk

TimeWarp's Stephanie Freeman with Richard O'Brien © David Freeman.

Chapter
05

Fishnet Economy: The Commerce of Costumes and *The Rocky Horror Picture Show*

Aubrey L. C. Mishou

→ It is early summer in Baltimore, and a man in green scrubs stands in front of a small bar, smoking a cigarette. He introduces himself as the organizer of the event, and ushers us inside, where the tight space has been transformed into a makeshift theatre: a projection screen hangs from the back of the stage, and rows of chairs have been arranged in front of a few remaining cocktail tables.

Figure 1: The MC of a Baltimore Rocky Horror costume contest modelling his costume homage to his former role as Dr Frank-N-Furter © Baxter Cohen.

'Magenta' is busy serving drinks, occasionally tilting her head to see through a mass of dark curls. Columbia sits at a small table to one side, her top hat glittering as she busily colours a Pabst Blue Ribbon poster to enter into the *Rocky Horror* art contest.

As the crowd grows, Brad and Janet walk hand-in-hand into the bar, find a table, and remove their clothes, spending the rest of the evening in bright white underwear. A table of Magentas celebrate the birthday of one with cupcakes in the shape of iconic red lips, a pants-less and fishnet-clad African American Professor Scott army-crawls across the floor with a teddy bear, and there's a sea of fishnets, leather and long feather boas. Two-thirds of the crowd have arrived in *Rocky Horror*-inspired garb to watch the first local public showing of *The Rocky Horror Picture Show* in several years, donning their finest black in celebration of the fandom that brings them together. When asked what constitutes appropriate fan costumes at *Rocky Horror* events, Ruth Fink-Winter, the *Rocky Horror* devotee behind the Anal Retentive Costume List says, '[It's] kinda the original "let your freak flag fly"'.

Fan costuming is an art most often defined by dedication demonstrated through the pursuit of authenticity – and that level of authenticity can come at a great cost. In 1999, *RHPS* fan Kim Shafer, exhausted by the search for the perfect sequined fabric for a Columbia bustier, takes extreme measures, and has the fabric custom-made. Initially, a single bolt is produced, and she sells the fabric to other *Rocky* costumers for $50 a yard. The investment seems great: fans who wear any size larger than a US size 6–8 will require at least a yard and a half, and those who are better endowed will want two yards for adequate sequinage. Yet Columbias deem the expense worth the cost, as can be determined by Shafer's sales: in less than two months her stock is depleted. However, the cost of the material does not necessarily denote its quality and functional use, as it lacks a lining – according to photos and reviews it is literally strings of sequins stitched together, rendering it useless for anything more than a decorative cover for a piece that still needs to be constructed. The total investment of this single item thus grows exponentially, as one begins to consider all of the materials, and time, necessary to fabricate the 'perfect' Columbia bodice. (Contemporary Columbias need not despair over Shafer's depleted stock – Larry of The Home of Happiness,

Fishnet Economy: The Commerce of Costumes and *The Rocky Horror Picture Show*
Aubrey L. C. Mishou

'in an effort to help the Rocky Horror world' has had the custom fabric duplicated, and continues to sell the material for $50 a yard.)

This expense of fandom, and the dedication to replication, can be great, both economically and emotionally; do-it-yourself custom costumes and original punk-inspired fashions are favoured over the oft-vilified commercial productions, and the minutia of mimicry comes at a far greater cost than the 'passing' licensed garb. This chapter seeks to explore costuming in the world of *Rocky Horror* fandom, considering the cost of authenticity and the conflict of creative expression and consumerism in regards to the competition of fandom. By examining fan costuming through the lens of contemporary costuming and cosplay, identifying its place in DIY culture, and determining the worth of cosplay as separate from traditional economic signifiers, the *worth* of fan costuming, excepting its monetary value, can be established.

Significant to an analysis of *Rocky Horror* costuming, is an understanding of costuming as a hobby and practice, and the history behind fan replication that leads to Bill O'Brien arriving at the Waverly, dressed as Dr Frank-N-Furter for a midnight screening of the cult classic.

Rocky fan costuming is nearly as old as midnight screenings, and the phenomenon developed no less organically than Louis Farse's first call-backs. According to Sal Piro in 'It Was Great When It All Began', *Rocky* fan costuming first appeared, appropriately, on Halloween, when movie fans arrived at the Waverly dressed as their favourite characters. But the phenomenon gained momentum in the spring of 1977, when Dori Hartley translated her fascination of 'Frank' into expression through costuming.

Figure 2: Twiggy Steele in the Frank-N-Furter costume she makes herself. 'One Halloween a few years back I wanted to be Dr Frank for Halloween but I sure as hell wasn't going to be paying for a costume – plus if you buy one it's made for men!!... The shirt was actually the hardest part... I knew that I couldn't just wear a corset it wouldn't give me the right look. I ended up Google image searching his shirt and found out how to make it [sic] © S. Baxter Cohen.

The more Dori saw the film, the more her obsession with Frank grew. First she dyed her blond hair black, then she had a permanent so she could have the exact hairdo that Frank has in the film. At her thirteenth viewing, she appeared wearing make-up identical to Frank's and a cape like his that she made herself. Outside, the crowd waiting in line applauded her. She was encouraged by the response, and worked constantly to improve her costume and make-up. It was Dori who re-introduced special clothing for the film and it was here to stay. (Sal Piro)

Inspired by the fan response to Dori, other fans began arriving in character guises; by the end of the six-month run, Hartley had amassed a costumed cast that included Frank, two Magentas, a Columbia and a Riff Raff.

By Piro's account, 14 year old Maria Medina's near-perfect Magenta costume inspired 'the first and most heated of the rivalries between fans wearing the same costume'. The second Magenta, Robin Lipner, was inspired by Medina's efforts, and sought to outdo her in impersonating Patricia Quinn's screen character. Piro's account lacks details on this purported rivalry, but does specify that Medina's impersonation was what inspired Lipner to complete her own costume, and have the confidence to wear it in public. Here, the work of costuming goes towards confidence-building in the act of fandom: though perhaps undecided before seeing Medina's work, the competitive fandom the other's costume incites allowed for greater confidence in Lipner's own expression of fandom, and of herself. Piro's narrative suggests that without this competition, Lipner may never have found the inspiration to finish her own costume, and may never have contributed to the phenomenon of fan costuming. This initial 'court' assembled by Hartley would serve as inspiration to other fan communities, and helped establish the discourse of costuming in *Rocky Horror* fandom. These 1977 costumes established *one* level of fan participation that will become an integral part of the true *Rocky Horror Picture Show* experience. Emboldened by the response to her costumes, Hartley began performing as Frank, eventually pantomiming the entire 'Sweet Transvestite' number on stage.

> As 1977 was ending, we were on top of the world and having the time of our lives. In our wildest imaginations, though, we never dreamed of the dramatic future lying ahead for the cult of RHPS audience participation. Already the media – newspapers, magazines, you name it – had begun to pick up on what was going on at the Waverly. (Sal Piro)

The practice of costuming, a term here used to describe both the hobby and profession of recreating fantastic media figures by means of crafting and sewing, is grounded in this landscape of 'fandom', particularly in the science fiction community. In 1939, Forrest J. Ackerman and Myrtle Jones first gained media attention for dressing in film-inspired costumes at the 1st World Science Fiction Convention in New York, says Dr. John L. Flynn in 'Costume Fandom: All Dressed Up With Someplace to Go' (1986). The interactive demonstration of interest and fandom soon caught on, and from Ackerman and Jones come twelve costumed conference attendees the next year, and numbers kept rising. Today, cosplay – the term used to describe fan costuming related to fantasy and science fiction conventions – has gained new notoriety, as event attendance booms and shows like *Heroes of Cosplay* (SyFy, 2013) give audiences a look at the process of designing and crafting (with, admittedly and unfortunately, a wealth of melodrama). In 2011, Eddie Walsh cited Oni Hartstein as saying, 'Costumes aren't just for Halloween and Cosplay isn't just a fad with teens, Cosplay is on the verge of becoming a major force

Fishnet Economy: The Commerce of Costumes
and *The Rocky Horror Picture Show*
Aubrey L. C. Mishou

in American pop culture'. This force is best defined in the same article, 'Cosplay Diplomacy', when Henry Lee of American Cosplay Paradise puts a clear price tag on what has become a booming industry: 'the industry has grown from practically nothing in the early-2000s to being worth about $5 million to $7 million per year, numbers [Lee] says are set to keep rising'. The interest in costuming is clearly growing, but what is less distinct in Lee's tallies is the level of audience participation within the cosplay and costuming communities. This 'industry' is supported less by pre-fabricated costumes, and more by the sale of accessories, materials, promotional materials and the events themselves.

Costuming as a contemporary hobby has its roots in the do-it-yourself movement, with one significant distinction: costumers are not invested in the thrift of traditional DIY crafters, and the authentic materials they seek help establish this growing commodity centre. Fans invested in authentic representation seek to create what is not available commercially, typically defined by a high level of faithfulness to original source materials, and the desire to demonstrate one's emotional investment in that source through the material homage of recreation. Costuming is a means of media consumption that allows fans to not only verbally and artistically profess dedication to a specific work, but also allows them to temporarily transcend the realities surrounding a text and become a part of its present. This transcendence is achieved not through purchasing 'the best' packaged Riff costume one can find, but in investing time, energy and attention to the construction of an identity that has value to the costumer.

Do-it-yourself guides to *The Rocky Horror Picture Show* are in abundance, and range from the casual Halloween party-goer to the more dedicated minutia researched by performers, who are best described as the most commercially and personally invested fans. The Anal Retentive Costume List, an archive of costuming details from fabrics to costume changes to make-up techniques, is one such source – and one to whom most other sources allude. Searching for the costumes in stores and on the Internet helps define the existence of these guides, and grounds the *Rocky* costuming phenomenon clearly in the realm of DIY. Why? Few pre-fabricated costumes are commercially available, and even fewer of these are admired for quality or authenticity. While veteran *Rocky* devotees such as Mina Credeur of Columbia's Closet and Ruth Fink-Winter of the Anal Retentive Costume List are diplomatic in response to my enquiries regarding these products, no doubt trying to preserve the spirit of acceptance integral to the *Rocky Horror* experience, the public consensus of the commercially available – and licensed – costumes are overwhelmingly censorious. Though these costumes are the only ones available (aside from used sales or custom costume pieces), and are reasonably priced, they do not satisfy the universal signifiers of 'good' *Rocky* costumes, lacking *both* emotional investment demonstrated by creative expenditures, *and* authenticity. The true value of a *Rocky Horror* costume is found in the emotional investment of the costumer, and not in the economic exchange of material goods.

The strongest primary sources for an analysis of *Rocky Horror* costuming, and what

Figure 3: Costumer Samantha Gibbs writes, 'The best piece I've made thus far would have to be Columbia's sequin tailcoat. It is a costume piece worn by all of the people who perform as Columbia in my cast. This piece holds a special place in my heart because I was able to be creative with it.' Photograph © Jennifer Springel.

is considered 'good', are the guidelines published by performance groups, and the costumes-as-texts created by fans themselves. Transvestite Soup in Minnesota provides a complex set of character-specific guidelines for aspiring cast members, distinguishing between 'Probationary', 'Minimum' and 'Fabulouuuus!' costumes. For each character, author Diana McCleery provides a list of garments and accessories, and offers the levels of emulation appropriate for a categoric distinction. For example, a 'Probationary' Columbia jacket is a tailcoat provided by the cast, 'if it fits you'. The description of a minimum-effort Columbia jacket is more specific:

I suggest you go ahead and get the nicest gold coat you can make/have made. Don't hesitate to ask for help from [a] director. Even a shitty gold-dot coat will be a hassle and not cheap. Unless it's entirely impossible, go ahead and bite the bullet and get real sequin fabric, but gold 'foil dot' is livable. Shitty, but liveable.

There are several elements of McCleery's description that are fruitful when considering the worth and expectations of participatory fan costuming. First is the emphasis on fan-made pieces: as opposed to directing aspiring Columbia's to a ready-made costume piece, McCleery recommends that the 'nicest gold coat' available is one that a performer 'can make/have made'. The expectation of DIY and custom costuming is clear in this statement, as the suggestion to make one's own Columbia jacket is foremost in the expectations of a *minimally* costumed cast member; that McCleery offers the suggestion to have a jacket *made* is an afterthought, as further emphasized through fabric recommendations – McCleery expects that the author will have a familiarity with material (knowing the difference between 'real sequin fabric' and 'foil dot'), and thus some level of costuming experience. Here, poor choices in material are deemed acceptable, expletively described as 'liveable', but clearly less than satisfactory. That a custom-made jacket, made with the 'wrong' material, could be deemed 'minimal' demonstrates the expectation of material dedication to the role, and the movie standards of the performance cast. It isn't enough to *resemble* Columbia; actors are expected to replicate all elements of her costume as closely as possible – and at nearly double the cost of the foil-dot fabric, the investment is not insignificant. (By comparison, the 'Fabulouuuus' Columbia jacket is described thus: 'Gold sequined coat, properly tailored. Boy, don't you look Fabulous!! And that's what being Columbia is all about. If you don't induce at least one epileptic seizure per show from all the Sparkly, your costume still needs work. ;)' [emphasis added].)

Fishnet Economy: The Commerce of Costumes
and *The Rocky Horror Picture Show*
Aubrey L. C. Mishou

Ranging from $16–$25 in 2014, the sequin fabric for the gold jacket may cost a costumer over $50 for the fashion fabric alone, not considering a lining (sequin fabric is, after all, fairly irritating), notions (thread, buttons, fasteners, interfacing and any other supplies that go into the construction of a sewing project), and an investment of time. By comparison, the licensed, five-piece Columbia costume sold around the web and popular in Halloween shops costs an average of $30, and perhaps a few days of shipping time.

Veteran costumer and entrepreneur Mina Credeur of Columbia's Closet offers an alternative vision to that espoused by Transvestite Soup, saying:

> I think there's room for 'all types'. Whether Columbia is wearing a skip-a-row gold sequin tailcoat with perfect black lapels – or just a metallic jacket from the thrift store – if it's consistent with their cast style I think it's all great. To throw on a plain black jacket and call it done is where the effort runs short. I've also seen a lot of costumes that intentionally deviate from the film – but they're amazing because the person has put so much effort – and so much of themselves – into it. I respect that a lot. There's a lot of room for interpretation and having fun with costumes. I just don't understand why you'd want to get up there in your street clothes.

Figure 4: A licensed Columbia costume, purchased from a US novelty store
© S. Baxter Cohen.

Ruth Fink-Winter echoes this sentiment regarding fan (attendee) costuming when she says:

> the whole thing about *Rocky* is going and being yourself and having a good time, which I know sounds really weird since a lot of us do that by saying, 'ok, I'm going to try to look exactly like these people from a 38-year-old-movie.

By these parameters, *Rocky Horror* fan costuming is not just about replication and mimicry – though it most devotedly takes this form, but also about one's level of personal investment in both the primary source and the expression of self. Thus, for the Pabst artist at the Baltimore show, a store-bought (and borrowed) costume is appropriate and applauded, expressing a casual level of fandom and an investment in the evening that supports the fandom defined by the event, if *not* the fan culture as a whole. For the true Columbia fan, however, the investment is only beginning with a properly-tailored old sequin tailcoat, and not every Columbia can afford it.

Figure 5: Robert Mrazik's Riff Raff Wig: 'The Riff Raff I built is made out of European materials, very strong and the best materials. The silk used on the top is the highest grade and costs about $375 a meter nowadays. Make-up can be applied right on top of the silk and everything can blend right into the actor's skin if it's done right. Quite often it is not and the actor looks like they are wearing a gag wig or something very cheap or bad [sic]'. The pictured wig is offered on Etsy for USD $1,450 © Robert Mrazik.

Despite this emphasis on personal construction of costumes, specialty costume accessories – those beyond the typical purview of tailors and crafters – remain highly prized, often with economic signifiers to indicate their rarity and value within the community. Two such items are wigs and footwear; the practices of wig-making and cobbling outside the most-often practised creative skills demonstrated by cosplay. Here, even experienced and dedicated costumers must turn to those with greater expertise, and specialists such as Robert Mrazik, and the custom shoe builders of Amazon Dry Goods fill the cosplay void.

According to Ruth Fink-Winter, hair is a topic of great consternation for *Rocky* cosplayers, because the distinctive coifs of the film are laborious to reproduce (when even marginally possible), and incredibly difficult to costume. On Anal Retentive, Fink-Winter recommends purchasing and styling commercially available wigs to achieve signature looks, offering tips on achieving colour and volume, and presenting matter-of-fact analysis regarding authenticity. In a personal interview, Fink-Winter claimed that her favourite costume piece is the USD $400 specialty space-wig she purchased to portray Magenta; for Fink-Winter, who does not identify as a seamstress and most frequently purchases her costume pieces, the cost of the wig is inconsequential due to its authenticity, though she recognized the expenditure may read as extravagant to those less involved. The price of the piece is of no surprise to wig maker Robert Mrazik, who understands the labour-intensive process of producing a materially-sound piece – and the necessity of such pieces for accurate *Rocky* portrayal. In an interview related to the Riff wig he is currently selling, Mrazik says:

> With Riff Raff the easiest thing to do is cast a guy who looks like Riff Raff... Not as easy as it sounds right. So now the illusion has to be created. In film it would take about 4 to 5 hours to make Riff come alive. First the actor's hair would be prepped to have a baldpate applied. All of his or her original hair is all tucked away and hidden in various ways. Then a baldpate of flesh is applied to look like they are bald, then the hair piece would go on top of that (probably about $3000 to $5000 for the piece). Time consuming and hugely expensive yes indeed.

So then, do expectations shift according to available financial expenditure? According to stage costumer Samantha Menyalion, yes:

> I know of many casts who have very strict rules about making their costumes as screen accurate as possible. These casts tend to be comprised of members who are more financially capable of affording all of the materials and pieces required to achieve this than my own shadow cast is. Considering the fact that a large amount of our members are college students, I guess you could say we are 'economically challenged'. Our main source for costuming items tends to come from thrift stores.

**Fishnet Economy: The Commerce of Costumes
and *The Rocky Horror Picture Show***
Aubrey L. C. Mishou

Occasionally we can save up for a certain item. We also have 'community pieces', which all members of the cast may use, when performing as a certain character. I've made several of these pieces for that purpose. However, what my cast may lack in 'authenticity', we make up for in creativity.

The worth of *Rocky Horror* fan costuming may best be illustrated by Ruth Fink-Winter, when she describes in a personal interview the $600 custom-made suede Victorian Magenta boots she had made in 2005 – the emphasis, here, being 'suede':

I am a non-leather wearing vegetarian. I don't own any leather shoes – except for the ones that I wear at *Rocky Horror*... My husband, slightly less of a non-leather wearing vegetarian than I am, wears a leather jacket of the correct style for Frank-N-Furter […] which probably includes half a cow. So for the floor show, yeah, he's wearing a bunch of dead furry animals around his neck. It's *Rocky Horror* – it doesn't count. We're lifers. ●

Figure 6: Ruth Fink-Winter's custom-made Victorian Magenta boots, purchased from Amazon Dry Goods for $600 in 2005. Ruth says, 'When I ordered them I'd been doing this for twenty years, so I figured chances were good I would get good wear out of them'. © Ruth Fink-Winter

~~~~~~~~~~~~~~~~

GO FURTHER

Online

'Cosplay Diplomacy'
Eddie Walsh
thediplomat.com,
http://thediplomat.com/2011/09/cosplay-diplomacy/. 2011.

'Costume Fandom: All Dressed Up With Someplace to Go!'
Dr John L. Flynn
http://www.costuming.org. 2005.

'It Was Great When It All Began'
Sal Piro
RockyMusic.com (n.d.), http://www.rockyhorror.com/history/howapbegan.php.

Costume Standards – Columbia
Diana McCleery
TransvestiteSoup.org (n.d.), http://www.transvestitesoup.org/sites/transvestitesoup.org/files/docs/costume-standards-Columbia.pdf.

Website

The Anal Retentive Costume List: http://www.rockyhorrorcostumelist.info/

Columbia's Closet: http://columbiascloset.blogspot.com

Fan Appreciation no. 4
Ruth Fink-Winter, BOSS Award Recipient

Interviewed by Marisa C. Hayes

Marisa C. Hayes (MCH): *You're involved with a number of* RHPS *fan sites and online resources. Can you tell us a little about your work for the various sites?*

Ruth Fink-Winter (RFW): I run the Anal Retentive Rocky Horror Costume List, which is exactly what it sounds like: a character-by-character listing of costumes, with reference photos and make-up schemes. We're in the middle of a revamp; the site was much more relevant before the DVD came out, giving everyone the ability to freeze frame. Some people still need some help figuring out what to look for, and it does keep me amused. These days I mostly work on sources and tips to help people put the costumes together.

I do the social media work for my *Rocky Horror* cast (most casts maintain a web presence; it's the easiest low-effort way to reach people or have them find you if they aren't reached by word of mouth). I also do some content for *RockyHorror.org*'s Facebook feed; I've still got a lot of connections from the days I ran a fanzine ('Crazed Imaginations') and I travel.

When the 'Rocky Horror Picture Show FAQ' was created, in the days of the *Rocky Horror* newsgroup, I used to send in content/corrections; I maintain and update its current incarnation, *Rockypedia.org*. We have a couple of other editors, but in the age of Google, while it's the primary source of information to a lot of queries, sometimes people don't realize that the origin is us. (When other websites use your exact text, you kind of know...). Occasionally I update Wikipedia's *Rocky Horror* entry when inaccuracies creep in.

In addition, I work with the folks from *RockyHorror.org*. Since the demise of the *Rocky Horror* newsgroup, the community's a little fragmented online. This provides a list of showings, articles and forums, and gives me someplace to put some of the things I'd have put in a paper fanzine back in the days I ran one. I loved running a paper fanzine, but the economics no longer work, and you can reach thousands online instead of a hundred people who want to hold a piece of paper with printing on it. So I'm still networking.

MCH: *You were a RHPS fan during the pre-Internet days; how has fandom changed for you with digital resources and the online community?*

RFW: I started *Rocky* before things went digital, but my non-digital period was very short; I got involved in the *Rocky Horror* newsgroup when it got started, perhaps my sophomore year in college. It was a lot harder to find information then, of course, and books were much more relevant and harder to find. Sal Piro and the Rocky Horror Picture Show Fan Club dispensed information, and people found each other at conventions. I was living in Nebraska when I first got started, so there was the one cast in the state and that was it. Word of mouth was very important; you'd hear there was *Rocky Horror* in Iowa and then go make some phone calls, figuring out who'd know how to get you enough information to go. The Internet has changed everything; I speak with friends I've never met, and when I do go someplace, I already know people there. I was able to run 'Crazed' from France, and when I found myself back in Nowhere, Iowa for work, it didn't matter; I was still connected. Even someone isolated like the young fan in Nebraska I was when I started can plug into the community. And it's much easier to meet fans from other countries, which has been amazing. The French in particular have really reached out to the rest of the community; they maintain a fantastic English/French website (http://www.sweet-transvestites.com/) and a lot of US fans have guested with them.

MCH: *In addition to your work for the online community, you're quite a world traveller. Can you tell us a little about your RHPS tourism?*

RFW: Most of my travel has been for work or school, though I've been to three of the UK conventions, because I could. People who play basketball reach out to folks who play basketball when they're in a foreign country. I do *Rocky Horror*. Of course, once you are abroad, when opportunities come up, you take them.

Probably the best experiences I've had include meeting up with a German friend (Peter Mendelsohn – he does Riff with the Berlin cast now), who was part of a troupe that did *The Rocky Horror Show*. He set up this amazing weekend – he got tickets to the European tour of *The Rocky Horror Show*, so we had a double weekend of his group's amateur production and the Eurotour in the Mannheim/Heidelberg area. My German's terrible, but he was very kind.

Seeing Oakley Court, where the film was made, with some Scottish and American friends after the Transylvania '99 Convention, was amazing. It's like a pilgrimage for a *Rocky Horror* fan; we stayed in the actual hotel and had tea in the ballroom the 'Time Warp' ballroom is modelled on. We were taking pictures of everything; the staff was lovely. Transylvania '99 blew the top of my head off; there were fans from as far away as Japan and Israel, and they had a lot of the Transylvanians, actors from the original play and subsequent productions/tours.

One of the Scottish performers, Marty Fairgrieve, also put on a convention in Manchester. It was amazing; people were buying Patricia Quinn (Magenta) drinks at the bar, and you might find yourself having breakfast at the hotel with one of the film's Transylvanians. Patricia and Perry Bedden came on as Riff and Magenta for the space scene. There's more of the casual mingling now at the US cons, but I'd never experienced it before. The original Rocky, Rayner Bourton, propositioned my husband, who was in full Frank gear. We think he was kidding but we're tickled either way.

When I was studying in Paris, I was able to take a trip to London to see *The Rocky Horror Show* put on professionally (I'd seen a small production in Kansas City, but this was the West End production with Anthony Head). That was how I celebrated my 21st birthday. I was similarly lucky when studying in Switzerland. The Fan Club mentioned that Richard O'Brien, the film/play's author and the original Riff Raff, was doing a one-man show in London. I figured I was most of the way there already, so I went. It was fabulous; he sang, he vamped, and he signed autographs afterwards. I ran into some other folks in the audience I later realized were from the Scottish cast.

While I was working in France in 2001, Marty was doing a charity showing in Manchester and invited me, and got me my first interview with Richard O'Brien, which was amazing (sitting at a table in a Manchester hotel, nibbling a scone while Richard O'Brien sang an excerpt of an early song, I simply couldn't believe where I was). The connections with the fanzine also netted me a couple of interviews while I was there; Sue Blane (the original *Rocky Horror* costumer), whom I'd met at Transylvania '99, contacted me and asked if I wanted to come interview her and see *Dance of the Vampires* in Germany. Heck, I knew the right answer to that! So I got on a train, got to meet the lady and see some of her costumes up-close. Christopher Malcolm also arranged for me to do some interviews at the Eurotour in Southern Germany.

Finally, travelling up to Paris, either when I was studying there, or taking the train from where I was working on the west Atlantic, and being received with open arms by the Paris cast just makes me smile. I've made the trip several times, and they were so wonderful and welcoming. These people had no reason to reach out to me, but we were fellow fans. When you are a *Rocky Horror* fan, you have friends in any city with a cast. It's a beautiful thing.

I've been delighted to interact with fans from other countries; plugging the work they do and their take on *Rocky Horror* was something I enjoyed a lot when I ran the fanzine. The Brits and the Scots are impacted

Fan Appreciation no. 4
Ruth Fink-Winter

by the fact that the play is touring there all the time; the Japanese take the same over-the-top colourful approach to *Rocky* that they take to everything; and the Germans are absolutely mad for the *The Rocky Horror Show*; the European tour pretty much tours the country, with occasional excursions to other countries, then back home to Germany. I speak a couple of languages, which helps, though many of the international fans speak English. I am so profoundly grateful that I've met wonderful people from so many countries. There's the French Riff/Magenta pair who wowed everyone at the 35th Anniversary with their glorious space outfits that she made. There's the nine-foot tall Dutch Frank, who performed on the Blu-ray (OK, maybe he was only seven feet in his heels). There's Marty, a Scottish Eddie, who throws conventions and owns one of the costumes from *Shock Treatment* (Jim Sharman, 1981). There are the Australian fans, only one of whom I've met in person. One out-dresses Divine and has amazing stories to tell about Sydney decadence; there's the gentleman who photographed the Max Phipps tours who shared Max's sketches of the show, as well as amazing ephemera and a photo archive that would make you cry. There's Mark Jabara, who runs the Australian *Rocky Horror* site (http://www.ozrockyhorror.com/), who's turned up productions of the show that some of us thought were only legend. There are the folks from TimeWarp (http://www.timewarp.org.uk/), the Official UK Fan Club, who know everything about the actors, maintain a giant sprawling website full of everything, and hold a picnic at Oakley Court every year. I'm sure I'm leaving someone out and I'm sorry. ●

Ruth Fink-Winter performing as Magenta © George of Midnight Madness.

Chapter
06

Performing Promiscuity: Female Sexuality, Fandom and *The Rocky Horror Picture Show*

Alissa Burger

→ One of the central conflicts of *The Rocky Horror Picture Show* is that of Janet Weiss and Brad Majors's respective sexual awakenings, triggered by the events at Frank-N-Furter's castle, and one of the great unanswered questions the film leaves viewers with as the credits roll are what the repercussions of that awakening and the newfound sexual knowledge of each will have on them, both separately and as a couple.

As we see in the 'Floor Show' segment, Brad and Janet have responded very differently to their experiences and their own responses to them: while Janet celebrates her increased confidence and the freedom she has found to explore and enjoy her sexuality, Brad is disturbed and perhaps even traumatized, literally crying out for his 'mommy'. The castle takes off to return to Transylvania, leaving Janet, Brad and Dr Scott writhing on the ground below, still clad in their corsets, fishnet stockings and heels. But what comes next? Now that they have been awakened to their desires and passions and have given in to both, what potential punishment awaits them as they face the challenge of becoming reincorporated into society?

Before we can begin to answer this question, it is necessary to acknowledge the well-known sexual double standard to which men and women are subjected. A sexually active young man, even one with multiple partners, is rarely vilified but is instead congratulated for his sexual prowess, developing a reputation as a stud, player or ladies' man. However, a similarly sexually active young woman faces an entirely different kind of reputation, that of the slut. Women's sexuality is policed by two dichotomous poles: the virgin and the whore, the good girl and the bad girl. For women, there is often very little middle ground between these two extremes; it is an either/or proposition. Women who fall outside the scope of normative sexuality – often associated with traditional gender roles, well-controlled sexuality and monogamy – have long been subjected to 'slut-shaming', through which women who deviate from the sexual norm are harshly punished, both in terms of reputation, marginalized social status and even real-life violence, including rape and sexual assault. Faced with the consequences of unconventional sexuality, it is the 'good girl' who is celebrated: traditionally feminine, deferential to her male partner, and abstaining from sexual activity until marriage.

At the beginning of *The Rocky Horror Picture Show*, Janet Weiss is just such a 'good girl', responding to and embodying the gendered expectations established by this dichotomous categorization of female sexuality. While the 1970s culture contemporary with *The Rocky Horror Picture Show* was one of liberation and an active women's movement that challenged these perceptions of gender, the film reaches back a couple of decades earlier, to the idealized and nostalgic 1950s. As Sue Matheson describes Janet's appearance in the film's opening scenes in her essay on Hollywood icons and *The Rocky Horror Picture Show*, Janet 'is a send up of the '50s suburban Puritan', in both her relationship and recent engagement to Brad, as well as her physical appearance and dress, as she '[embodies] the sexual double standard for women during the 1950s […] dressed in a conservative white hat that covers her head in church and a modest mauve suit buttoned to her neck that shows off her legs above the knees'. As Matheson argues, Janet is 'the nice girl next door, who supports the power of patriarchy and its values'. This 1950s ideal of purity and the contrasting fear of being labelled a 'slut' worked to keep girls and women within the accepted bounds of traditional and respected femininity. As Leora Tanenbaum explains in her book *Slut! Growing Up Female with a Bad Reputation* (2000):

Performing Promiscuity: Female Sexuality, Fandom and *The Rocky Horror Picture Show*
Alissa Burger

Figure 1: Brad and Janet's embrace of traditional gender roles, in both relationship and attire © Twentieth Century Fox

For girls who came of age in the 1950s, the fear of being called a slut ruled their lives. In that decade, 'good' girls strained to give the appearance that they were dodging sex until marriage. 'Bad' girls – who failed to be discreet, whose dates bragged, who couldn't get their dates to stop – were dismissed as trashy 'sluts.' Even after she had graduated from high school, a young woman knew that submitting to sexual passion meant facing the risk of unwed pregnancy, which would bar her entrée into the social respectability of the college-educated middle class. And so, in addition to donning cashmere sweater sets and poodle skirts, the 1950s 'good' girl also had to hone the tricky talent of doling out enough sexual preliminaries to keep her dates interested while simultaneously exerting enough sexual control to stop before the point of no return: intercourse.

These sexual expectations, including that the woman will be – or at least ought to be – a virgin on her wedding night is underscored in the opening scene of *The Rocky Horror Picture Show*, with the aftermath of Betty Munroe and Ralph Hapschatt's wedding, including the shaving cream message on the newlyweds' car that 'she got hers, now he'll get his'. As the film begins, this is the female sexuality that Janet has been socialized to and embraces; as she later tells Rocky in 'Touch-a, Touch-a, Touch Me', she has 'only ever kissed before' and that 'heavy petting' could only lead to trouble.

However, once Janet and Brad arrive at Frank-N-Furter's castle, she begins to discover – and delight in – the untapped potential and pleasure of her own sexuality. Initially, Janet resists the sexual decadence of Frank-N-Furter's castle, clinging to her 'good girl' persona and begging Brad to get them out of there, to take her away to somewhere less 'unhealthy', someplace more safe and wholesome. When she and Brad are undressed by Riff Raff and Magenta, Janet's underwear is shown to be just as prim and proper as the rest of her image, with virginally white bra, underwear and half-slip; though her body is to some extent revealed, her 'charming underclothes' (as Frank remarks) are the lingerie of a 'good' girl, a properness underscored by the fact that she continues to wear her pantyhose and white shoes, as well as carry her white pocketbook from the castle's hall to Frank's lab and her bedroom beyond. Janet is horrified by the excess they find within the castle, seeking immediate escape as she drags Brad backwards toward the door during the 'Time Warp' and later, in Frank's lab, when she is introduced to Rocky, who Jeffrey Weinstock calls 'libido personified' in his 2007 book on the film, she shrinks demurely away, blushingly telling Frank that 'I don't like men with too many muscles'. However, Janet's resistance doesn't hold for long and is in fact already beginning to slip in Frank's lab when she giggles and flushes at Frank's flirtations, declares herself only minutes later to be 'a muscle fan', and speculatively appraises Frank, Rocky and Eddie.

Janet enacts both resistance and regret when she realizes it is Frank who has come to her bedroom and into her bed, rather than Brad, telling him 'you tricked me! I wouldn't

Figure 2: Brad and Janet's
'charming underclothes'
Twentieth Century Fox.

have!' In tears, she laments that 'I was saving myself', a phrase which underscores the notion of women's sexuality as currency, with their virginity defining their worth, both as individuals and as commodities within the marriage market. This belief that a girl or woman is inherently devalued following the loss of her virginity is still alive and well in abstinence-only sexual education and current cultural perceptions, particularly in the United States. As Jessica Valenti explores in her 2010 book *The Purity Myth: How America's Obsession with Virginity is Hurting Young Women*:

> While boys are taught that the things that make them men – good men – are universally accepted ethical ideals, women are led to believe that our moral compass lies somewhere between our legs. Literally. Whether it's the determining factor in our 'cleanliness' and 'purity', or the marker of our character, virginity has an increasingly dangerous hold over young women. It affects not only our ability to see ourselves as ethical actors outside of our own bodies, but also how the world interacts with us through social mores, laws, and even violence.

Frank takes a more liberating perspective on female sexuality as potentially limitless and constantly replenishing, inviting Janet to embrace her own pleasure with his observation that 'I'm sure you're not spent yet'. Though this perspective creates a more positive potential for female sexuality in general and Janet's desire in particular, within the cultural understanding of women's sexuality as a commodity, Janet is 'damaged goods' and what is done cannot be undone.

After this token resistance, she gives herself over to Frank, pulling him into her bed and following her desires further into her own sexual exploration, quickly slipping along the dichotomous teeter-totter from virgin to slut, good girl to bad. Within the mythology of the slut, this initial sexual encounter, the loss of Janet's virginity and thus, more symbolically, her virtue, is irredeemable and as Matheson explains, Janet 'discovers a voracious sexual appetite that she proceeds to satisfy [...] Once "bitten" she becomes a fallen woman – a Lilith who joins her seducer in seeking and destroying others' sexual innocence'. With this single act, Janet is transformed and through her desire and sexuality, Matheson argues, 'her appetites have become aberrant. Wanting blood, she has become something alien, socially abhorrent, immoral, and un-American – a vampire', literally becoming monstrous as a result of her desire and, even more unforgivably, her enthusiastic embrace of that desire and her active choice to fulfill it.

Janet becomes voracious, indiscriminate, ruled by her sexual desire: a slut. She flees her room, stumbling across the injured Rocky in Frank's lab, where she takes ownership of her own sexuality, becoming an agent of her own desire as she seduces Rocky. Tending to Rocky's wounds, Janet considers the new possibilities of her awakened sexuality, a smile slowly spreading across her face, a smile which Kristin Watkins-Mormino argues

Performing Promiscuity: Female Sexuality, Fandom and *The Rocky Horror Picture Show*
Alissa Burger

'signals the completion of the process of defloration Frank began and unwittingly fostered but fail to control'. As Watkins-Mormino concludes, 'Janet's true sexual maturation occurs not when she surrenders her corporal virginity but when she recognizes and pursues her own fantasies'. In her song, 'Touch-a, Touch-a, Touch Me', she publicly proclaims this desire, revelling in her wantonness as she tells Rocky, 'I wanna be dirty'. While Janet gave herself to Frank, arguably in her encounter with Rocky, she is the one doing the taking, the one calling the shots; her seduction of Rocky may be amateurish, unpractised and even a bit humorous, with Magenta and Columbia laughing as they watch on the castle's television set, but Janet is demonstrating clear choice and agency, making her own sexual decisions and pursuing her own pleasure unbound by the traditional constraints of femininity, heterosexual relationships and the end-game of marriage preached by 1950s gender norms and rules. As Janet's sexuality becomes increasingly unbound so does her body, as she rips off sections of her slip to bind Rocky's wounds, further exposing her body along with her desires. However, Janet's newfound deviance and her embrace of it is perhaps most clearly illustrated in the 'creature of the night' refrain of 'Touch-a, Touch-a, Touch Me'. As Sarah Artt analyzes this sequence in her essay on *The Rocky Horror Picture Show* and the self-reflexive musical tradition, it is 'shot from Janet's perspective under Rocky as they make love, and she appears to be imagining other characters in Rocky's position: Brad, Frank, Magenta, Riff Raff, Columbia, and finally Rocky', her immediate sexual partner. She has not only had sex with Frank and now Rocky, but her desire is unbridled, all-encompassing and indiscriminate, if only in her fantasies (though these fantasies will be fulfilled, at least in part in the final 'Floor Show' segment, where Frank, Brad, Rocky, Columbia and Janet 'swim the warm waters of sins of the flesh' in Frank's pool). Awakened to her own desire, Janet is now controlled by that desire, having given herself over to her own pleasure and sexuality.

While Janet's discovery of her sexual potential has been a liberating experience, Brad's response is much different. As Matheson points out, just as Janet embodies a nostalgia-tinged 1950s femininity, Brad is '[m]odelled after the 1950s emotionless, heterosexual, hypermasculine hero [...] [who] embodies clean-living and God-fearing American values'. In their first moments at Frank-N-Furter's castle, while Janet tells Brad they need to leave, he continues to believe he is in control of the situation, reassured in his presumed knowledge that his perspective is just and right and, as a result, must eventually prevail. Even as he and Janet find themselves being undressed and led more deeply into the castle, he attempts to calm Janet, telling her that 'we'll play along for now and pull out the aces when

Figure 3: Janet's smile reflects her sexual awakening and growing agency © Twentieth Century Fox.

Figure 4: Janet shedding her clothing and sexual inhibitions © Twentieth Century Fox.

Figure 5: Janet's exploration and celebration of her sexuality – her 'mind has been expanded' © Twentieth Century Fox.

Figure 6: Back to reality and an uncertain future Twentieth Century Fox.

the time is right'. However, Brad's control of the situation – which was tenuous and self-delusional at best – slips ever further from him, as does his control over himself, his body and his desires. In his Freudian reading of the film, Raymond Ruble argues that both Brad and Janet

embark on an unwitting quest to discover their own sexuality. Brad represents the failure of this process to reach a healthy conclusion [...] Brad refuses to recognize that he has dynamic sexual desires, and at the film's conclusion is a ruined person obviously in need of psychoanalytic therapy.

In contrast, as Ruble continues, Janet 'represents a healthy adjustment to her newfound sexuality [...] Unlike Brad, she is capable of growing into a complete, healthy personality following the liberating experiences provided by Frank'. Brad and Janet's different responses to their experiences at Frank's castle are most clearly demonstrated in the song 'Rose Tint My World', where Janet celebrates the fact that her 'confidence has increased' and her 'mind has been expanded', while Brad quakes, fights his sexual urges, and cries for his mother.

However, the easy acceptance of Janet's newfound sexuality within the isolated confines of the castle will not carry back into the outside world and when it comes to leaving the castle, she and Brad face similar uncertainties and challenges. Judged by the morality of the larger culture and its valuation of female sexuality, Janet is 'ruined' and her new identity as a slut will be recast as destructive rather than liberating. As Weinstock points out, Janet's 'transformation from virgin to whore is a familiar Western cautionary tale in which one sexual indiscretion on her part awakens overwhelming, carnal desire'. Once discovered, Janet cannot now ignore or limit her sexual appetites, cannot return to being a 'good girl', and as a result, will find it difficult if not impossible to reintegrate herself into the larger society. For his part, Brad has been traumatized, forced to the realization that the white, masculine, heterosexual worldview that he had always taken for granted as the dominant one, the one which would shape the world in which he lives, is not as all-powerful as he has believed and taken for granted. The lyrics of 'Super Heroes' echo with destruction ('bleeding'), consumption ('feeding') and a powerful sense of loss. As Artt argues of 'Super Heroes':

The dark tone of the final song dispels the myth of integration [...] *Rocky Horror* shows us that Brad and Janet are no longer enveloped in Frank's paradise of sexual freedom, and as the lyrics of 'Super Heroes' imply, they will now have to deal with the

**Performing Promiscuity: Female Sexuality, Fandom
and *The Rocky Horror Picture Show***
Alissa Burger

deeper ramifications of their experiences.

Finally, as the end credits roll, the reprise of 'Science Fiction/Double Feature' tells viewers that 'Darkness has conquered Brad and Janet'. As Watkins-Mormino argues of these final two songs:

> It is safe to say, then, that their experience has had a negative effect on their future lives [...] Because their introduction into sexual maturity was removed from and in defiance of their own community, it is doubtful that their newfound status will allow them to assume their new roles harmoniously within Denton.

Brad and Janet's sexual experiences have occurred within the isolated microcosm of Frank's castle, but now they must be thrust back out into the real world, with its restrictive values and well-established gender roles and expectations, as well as both implicit and explicit punishment for deviation from these norms.

The Rocky Horror Picture Show and Janet's unfettered exploration of her sexuality within are a fantasy, a space within which she and the fans that identify with her at countless midnight showings are safe to embrace and enact these desires. James B. Twitchell argues that the message of *The Rocky Horror Picture Show* regarding female sexuality is that 'it is okay for girls to be naughty and dirty, to be sexual, bisexual, transsexual – you name it, as long as you enjoy it. Or perhaps to be more accurate, it is okay to *pretend* to be this way' (original emphasis). Within the darkened theatre, within Frank's castle and the insular world created by *The Rocky Horror Picture Show*, even as countless midnight-show audiences yell 'slut' when she appears on-screen, Janet's sexuality is celebrated. However, as we know from the accounts of Tanenbaum and others, the sexual freedom of the slut is not as enthusiastically embraced in the real world. As Thomas G. Endres writes of the decadent revelry celebrated by *The Rocky Horror Picture Show*, 'Eventually, the audience must go home. The makeup comes off, the costumes are put away for another late-night outing, and we return to our simple and practical lives'. Frank's castle, the film, the theatre, the exploration of women's sexuality outside the norms and values of the dominant culture: these are spaces that are separate from the viewers' real, everyday lives, and all the more fulfilling because of that separation.

The Rocky Horror Picture Show creates a space free from slut-shaming, one within which female sexuality and agency are celebrated, and this is a space that is desperately needed, especially given the reality that cultural perceptions and acceptance of women's sexuality have not changed dramatically in the forty years since the film's original release. ●

~~~~~~~~~~~~~

GO FURTHER

Books

Reading Rocky Horror: 'The Rocky Horror Picture Show' and Popular Culture
Jeffrey Andrew Weinstock (ed.)
(New York: Palgrave Macmillan, 2008)

The Purity Myth: How America's Obsession with Virginity is Hurting Young Women
Jessica Valenti
(Berkeley: Seal Press, 2010)

Slut! Growing Up Female with a Bad Reputation
Leora Tanenbaum
(New York: Perennial, 2000)

Extracts/Essays/Articles

'Dr. Freud Meets Dr. Frank N. Furter'
Raymond Ruble
In Donald Palumbo (ed.). *Eros in the Mind's Eye: Sexuality and the Fantastic in Art and Film* (New York: Greenwood Press, 1986), pp. 161–68.

'Frankenstein and the Anatomy of Horror'
James B. Twitchell
In *Georgia Review*. 37: 1 (1983), pp. 41–84.

Chapter
07

Philosophical Currents Through Film: *The Rocky Horror Picture Show*

Reuben C. Oreffo

→ The 1975 musical concoction of comedic horror and mock sci-fi that is *The Rocky Horror Picture Show (RHPS)* exemplifies a cultural artefact that, whilst not explicitly engaging with standard philosophical questions as part of the narrative, can be engaged with so as to begin thinking about the world in a more philosophical manner. Of course, it must first be clarified what is to be meant by 'philosophy'.

I subscribe to the Wittgensteinian perspective of the nature of philosophy, under which philosophy is understood to be an activity. Instead of digging deeper, philosophy 'just puts everything before us, and neither explains nor deduces anything. Since everything lies open to view there is nothing to explain'. Philosophy presents us with knots that are to be teased loose through the study of the language involved. A philosophical problem, according to Wittgenstein, 'has the form: "I can't find my way about"', and the philosopher is landed with the task to 'show the fly the way out of the fly-bottle'. This may seem at odds with some common notions of philosophy. Nevertheless, where philosophy may subsist on the clarification of ideas, there are undoubtedly perennial questions of all schools and traditions stretching back millennia that may be considered in conjunction with cultural artefacts. In studying the film through the course of this essay, I seek to offer some insight and stimulate thought regarding *RHPS*. More specifically I will show the capacity for engagement with philosophical notions of 'reality' and 'representation'.

Philosophers from the time of Aristotle through to Wittgenstein and Russell have differed in perspectives regarding the question of distinctions between thought which is said to correspond to reality, coherent abstractions, and that which cannot be thought of rationally. It is the branch of philosophy known as *metaphysics* which is said to be concerned with reality. Metaphysics forms the groundwork for many key areas of inquiry in philosophy. Generally speaking, metaphysics concerns itself with *how the world is*. By and large, metaphysics is concerned with questions regarding existence, possibility, free will, cause and effect, identity, substance and attribute, space and time, and many other questions; for example, the philosophy of mind. It is unclear where metaphysics finds its limits, and its definition being so obscure may lead us to try to understand it simply through encountering its questions. The terms of determinism, free will, dualism, materialism and idealism are all attributed to the vocabulary of metaphysics.

Delineating 'reality' and 'representation'

While we do not intend to complete a metaphysical inquiry, *RHPS* can be analysed to begin a consideration of something deeper with respect to representation and our beliefs concerning reality. A pivotal observation one can first make is the presence of multiple layers, abstracting characters from one another and the viewer from events: we are presented initially with narration and subsequently with further layers within the content of the story. We move from what we would refer to as a more 'realistic' series of events (the wedding, the breakdown of a car), to the comically *unconventional* world of Dr Frank-N-Furter. We become further removed as we view characters' observation of one another via television screens or from afar, finding ourselves perceiving characters through such layers. The film offers a superb exposition of the lack of concrete division between that which is called 'reality' and that which is typically referred to as 'unreality'.

What can be meant by 'reality' or 'representation'? We may note that the study of

Philosophical Currents Through Film: *The Rocky Horror Picture Show*
Reuben C. Oreffo

other linguistic traditions has demonstrated how it is seldom that every word in a language can be matched up to a corresponding word in another. Indeed, the differences between some languages are so great that we can reasonably concede that the way in which we interpret the world is somewhat different to someone with another language. As we divide up our world, the tools, including language, which we use, inevitably influence the partitions, our language surely shaping the way in which we look at the world. We use words to refer to things, though our words cannot be said to have an inner 'essence' prior to their use in context. Words do not refer to things, *people* do. This is rigorously explored, and more eloquently expressed, in P. F. Strawson's 'On Referring' (1950). 'Real' accordingly should not be thought of as having some built-in meaning, but a meaning assigned by the way in which it is used. In studying our own use of such terminology in the context of *RHPS*, I hope to make inferences regarding the wider use and understanding of these and related terms. One use of the term 'reality' is used to mark a sense of certainty and security in perception. Consider the following quote from Janet: 'I feel released / Bad times deceased / My confidence has increased / Reality is here'.

Reality is seen to have strong links to our idea of representation. When we represent something, we do not explicitly describe what it is, but instead say something *about* it. We do this through constructing something new, which exists *just as much* as that which it represents. In the context of a film, we produce new images and can form layers, as in *RHPS*, but these are nevertheless essential components to our reality simply by being presented to us. *RHPS* embodies an ideal microcosm in which we observe the construction of a reality; narratives are built within one another and we are tossed back and forth between these internal levels. We naturally feel there to be a solid demarcation criterion by which one may sort real phenomena from everything else, but this is to forget that key truism – that the reference for such a word as 'real', and hence its capacity to cut through the world, so to speak, lies in our public use of it. One finds the search for necessary and sufficient conditions for the property of 'realness' reduced to trivial futility, and we are reminded of this in the conflict rising out of considering whether elements of *RHPS* are real.

We find a translation of images and messages in different media and forms, such as video screens, the narrator's book and implication. All of these offer representations of other parts of reality. We can observe that, described independently, a television screen such as one representing events within the narrative of *RHPS* is indubitably seen as a 'real' object, a part of what we call reality. Yet in discussion, the images presented may be held to be less real than the encounter of the depicted forms. It is here that we see a falling through of demarcation – we act as if there are external criteria determining the 'realness' of an object, but it is the context that governs the meaning in language. Our language (in the broadest use of the term) defines the bounds to that which we can know.

Levels of abstraction

The work endlessly confronts us with means of representation and we instinctively perceive these to be different levels of reality. The engagement that one feels is key to the film and can be understood as integral to its gaining of cult status. Audience participation is something for which *RHPS* is renowned. Furthermore, the engagement goes further than the element of narration in the film. There are very clear ways by which *RHPS* brings about awareness of our connectedness to it and our role as spectator. The consolidation of the different levels of reality unifies the full production, such that it is not simply a succession of disparate scenes, but a coordinating work of which we are part. The narrator, or 'criminologist' (who we expect to be separate from the story he narrates), partakes in the music and some of the dialogue of the story, which helps neatly bind the work together. This is not to say that an element of time and completion is absent from the film. The narrator clearly moves through a book (see Figure 1) which is a fundamental tool for representing much of the film. The book gives us a sense of the finite nature of the narrative. Reconsidering our rational engagement with the film, we not only see the links between the components of the film and our watching of it, but the system as a whole.

Within the mechanism of *RHPS*, we see the establishment of different levels of abstraction from events. Throughout much of *RHPS*, we are aware of individuals being watched, characters witnessing others on cameras and responding to their behaviour. If we were to take a step back from the work for just a moment, we would find ourselves engrossed in the effort to decipher what is essentially the interplay within a plethora of layers:

- A sequence of events as audio-visual information captured on film
- The collated work presented as an artefact
- The performance of a cast of actors located on a film set
- A story narrated by a character named 'the criminologist'
- The fictional narrative of a couple caught up in a strange world
- The events ascertained by characters whilst somehow dislocated (in spying through various devices or observing through a medium)
- Clandestine implication in the script, especially sexual euphemism, and the imaginings/confusions of the characters within the story

This presents a simplified model of some integral parts of *RHPS*. What can be appreciated is this division and the clear interplay that gives the work its coherency. We are able to sketch out an interconnected system by which, for example, a character will sing and others will repeat (consider the monotone repetitions of 'Janet' in unison, or of 'down, down, down'). The key way that *RHPS* provides representation is in the repetition. Most notably, this is found in music in which the words of a given singer are mimicked by

Philosophical Currents Through Film: *The Rocky Horror Picture Show*
Reuben C. Oreffo

Figure 3: Clear division: a screen transition as we are returned to our narrator who shepherds us through the story © Twentieth Century Fox.

others. Full choruses are developed in *RHPS* in which the members are joined into a community. We find the repetition of music to be fundamental in holding the narrative together. Take for example the chorus line, 'in just seven days, I can make you a man' which is cut off mid-way and which then resurfaces to draw an end to the scene; being reasserted following its interruption distinctly has a sense of the restoration of order. The repetitions of *RHPS* constitute opportunities for other characters to appropriate the words and melodies of others in the production of music.

Beyond the narration, the clear division of scenes helps remind us of the production process which has gone into the making of the film. A scene ends, and we are delivered once again into the care of the narrator or issued forth to a contrasting series of events. We become aware of being guided through the film and this boosts our engagement. Occasionally, characters erupt from the confines of their level of reality to provide us with commentary. Consider, for example, the moment where Dr Scott turns to look into the camera and speaks of his nephew Eddy, 'I knew he was in with a bad crowd, but it was worse than I imagined'. This statement penetrates the layers between the narrative and us. What is more, our acknowledgement of implications being made throughout the work, such as those among certain jokes, help draw us in through forcing us to use our critical faculties in making the inference. One is reminded of Frank's response in the following interchange over dinner:

Dr Scott: We came here to discuss Eddie.
Columbia: Eddie!
Frank: That's a rather tender subject. Another slice anyone?

This revelation of cannibalism is among the more witty illustrations of Frank's acetic wit. *RHPS* shows the role of *conversational implicature* in day-to-day speech – meaning there is a gap between what is *said* and what is actually *meant* in conversation. Implication is a huge element of the film, constituting one of the most important comedic devices in *RHPS*. The film is fraught with euphemism, particularly of a sexual nature, and our filling in of the gaps is one of the most rewarding aspects to the film, our engagement facilitating the revelation of the meaning of each joke (which all too often displays a dark interior). The reward comes in the understanding of such jokes and is frequently confirmed through future events to which the jokes refer.

Connectedness and cause
The unity achieved in *RHPS* is not solely derived from these instances of engagement. In experiencing a work such as *RHPS*, we become part of the system. We must acknowledge our perception and subsequent reaction to be an output of the film. Causality is a strong theme in *RHPS*. We can see strong notions regarding causation throughout *RHPS* shown in expectation, explanation and prediction of certain events, all of which

Figure 4: Wide-eyed Janet
in the long pause of 'antici...
pation'. Is she justified
in predicting the word's
completion? © Twentieth
Century Fox.

are successfully demonstrated in the following from Frank:

So – come up to the lab,
And see what's on the slab.
I see you shiver with antici...pation.
But maybe the rain
Is really to blame.
So I'll remove the cause.
But not the symptom.

In the above, we see an instance of the treatment of causation. The huge three-second pause within 'anticipation' is cued with a wide-eyed expression (see Figure 3 of Janet), demonstrating the human prediction of events.

Reference is then made to the reason for (the cause of) the couple's wet condition following their entry from the rain. The more we consider causality throughout *RHPS*, the more we must ask in what *manner* such causality exists: do we ourselves construct it? The British philosopher David Hume certainly recognized the perception of causality to be an inescapable component of human thought. Hume argues that we cannot establish causal relations a priori (prior to experience) as we can effortlessly imagine the perceived cause taking place without its effect (without logical contradiction). What we hence resort to is that which he calls 'probable reasoning', by which we make our inferences. Hume maintains that such probable reasoning is independent of a previous 'operation of the mind', instead constituting an *instinct*. He confidently states in his *Treatise* (1738) that 'reason is nothing but a wonderful and unintelligible instinct in our souls'.

Immanuel Kant claimed in the preface to his *Prolegomena* (1783) the following effect of Hume's critical treatment of causality in metaphysics: 'it was the remembrance of David Hume which, many years ago, first interrupted my dogmatic slumber and gave my investigations in the field of speculative philosophy a completely different direction'. Kant went further to postulate his transcendental theory in which he claimed that causality, as well as other fundamental elements in reality (such as time and space) formed integral parts to our experience of the world. These elements originate from (are projected by) human beings, our experience of things (the *phenomena*) arising from the synthesis of ourselves and the world of which we are part. There are the things in and of themselves (the *noumena*) but which we cannot know, finding ourselves to be experiencing our world under irrepressible filters such as causality. What Kant builds up is an essential divide within his conception of reality in his ideas of the transcendental. Observing artefacts, such as *RHPS*, allows us to be wholly cognisant of perception itself, the film presenting an excellent exposition of the filters that lie between an event and our experience of it.

Philosophical Currents Through Film: *The Rocky Horror Picture Show*
Reuben C. Oreffo

Dream and reality

In discussing the matter of reality and its linked components we naturally continue to search for demarcations. Dream is one realm that we hold as escaping reality. The unusual course of events and the bizarre characters of *RHPS* would lead many to assert the work's dreamlike nature. Some valuable comparisons between the film and dream can be made: expression of emotion is often significantly exaggerated; the narrative takes sudden steps and events take place very suddenly without a gradual development towards them. Indeed, this interpretation of *RHPS* would be supported by the wedge the narrator embodies between us and the story.

Dream constitutes an outwardly significant concept in the understanding of our reality: it is believed to imitate reality, rather than to constitute a part of reality. Indeed, sceptical dream hypotheses have been made to not only reject our claim to reality in sleep, but to deny us knowledge, whether in dream or not. One is reminded of the final dream sequence of the film preceding the execution of Frank-N-Furter, the applauding crowds dissipating to reveal that which we would denote as the real state of things.

Even if we scrutinize the divide one attempts to make between reality and dream, we can appreciate distinctions that can be made and which are fundamental to the assertion that a dream is not real. When one dreams that X is taking place, it may reasonably be held that it is questionable where X is in fact taking place, yet we must not be hasty to hold that there is any necessary connection between what we call actual events and our waking interpretations. The distinction, which many would use as a means of differentiating between reality and 'unreality' in this context, is even made in *RHPS*: 'Don't dream it, be it'. This hedonistic imperative to act on your desires rather than simply dreaming of them reminds us of a clear distinction between dreaming an action and performing it.

In this, we are presented with another query that is philosophically interesting. Whilst *RHPS* doesn't itself provide philosophical arguments, the philosophically-relevant thoughts elicited regarding representation, reality, abstraction and causation can be exciting.

How one *engages* with certain ideas determines whether the activity is philosophical (whilst the very notion of any content being 'innately philosophical' is deemed suspect). What we can certainly acknowledge in *RHPS* are some engrossing abstract notions which drive to the heart of wider human experience. Progressing through the film, we come to see how despite the repetition and the segmentation of events, a coherent whole is still provided. Ultimately, what may make this film unique is its capacity to confront us with thoughts of such abstract notions through an erratic progression of events. Our common-sense notions of the boundaries between reality and 'unreality' are questioned and we become increasingly aware of how nothing experienced can be said to be 'pure' in the sense that we describe that which we deem real to be 'pure' – free from distortion, separation or obfuscation. Through systematically studying elements in works such

Figure 5: As if from out of dream: the castle takes off into the evening sky © Twentieth Century Fox.

as *The Rocky Horror Picture Show*, we can become aware of questions that may be asked which go far beyond the immediate narrative or image. Engagement with such artefacts lends us a ladder we are able to climb down to reach an end state of abstraction, under which philosophy thrives. ●

GO FURTHER

Books

An Introduction to the Philosophy of Language
Michael Morris
(Cambridge: CUP, 2013)

Metaphysics
Peter van Inwagen
(Boulder: Westview, 2004)

Prolegomena to Any Future Metaphysics
Immanuel Kant (trans. and ed. Gary Hatfield)
(Cambridge: CUP, 2004; rev. edn)

A Treatise of Human Nature (1739–40)
David Hume (ed. E. C. Mossner)
(Harmondsworth: Penguin, 1969)

Extracts/Essays/Articles

'On Referring'
P. F. Strawson
In *Mind*, New Series. 59: 235 (1950), pp. 320–344.

Online

'Metaphysics.' *Stanford Encyclopedia of Philosophy*, 10 September 2007, http://plato.stanford.edu/entries/metaphysics/.

Fan Appreciation no. 5
Jim 'Cosmo' Hetzer, Webmaster; and Bill Brennan,
Fanfiction Writer

Interviewed by Marisa C. Hayes

Marisa C. Hayes (MCH): *One of the unique features of your site,* Cosmo's Factory *(www.cosmosfactory.org), is its sizable fanfiction section that showcases how* RHPS *has a life outside the movie theatre through the written word. How did the fanfiction section come about?*

Jim 'Cosmo' Hetzer (JH): Early on people used to just e-mail it to me because there were no other *Rocky Horror* websites. And after a while I just became a repository for it. I was always open to displaying the work of others because I know how much some of the authors worked on it and the pride they took in writing.

MCH: *Do you receive a lot of fanfiction?*

JH: I received a great deal of it early on. It was something a fan could do in those pre-Photoshop days. Now anyone can make a flyer or a blog or something, but back in the early 1990s, fanfiction and fanart were two things people could do to show how much of a fan they were.

MCH: *I noticed that Bill Brennan has written a lot of* RHPS *fanfiction; is he partially responsible for launching the film's fanfiction movement?*

JH: I think Bill and I became friends early on because of all of the fanfiction he wrote and submitted. He was by far the king of it. He would send me stuff and we'd get to talking back and forth. About ten years ago he mailed me a big package of all of his handwritten fanfiction and artwork. I have an entire file-cabinet drawer filled with it.

MCH: *Bill, you've written so much fanfiction. Are you a writer by day? Or did fanfiction become a unique outlet to express your appreciation for the films?*

Bill Brennan (BB): I am not a writer by profession. I would no doubt starve. I am a manager of a gift shop in New Jersey. Fanfiction did indeed become an outlet for my *RHPS* and *Shock Treatment* (Jim Sharman, 1981) fandom. Like all fanfiction, it stems from the love of the characters in the films… I simply do not want the story to end! But since *Rocky Horror* and *Shock Treatment* do indeed have definite endings, I and people like me, take it upon ourselves to 'keep the characters alive' as it were.

MCH: *Do you write any other types of fanfiction?*

Fan Appreciation no. 5
Jim Hetzer

BB: It's a difficult question to answer. Most of my fanfiction involves 'cross-over' fiction, which is the blending of two films/plots/characters together. A good example would be *The Hunger Games*. I'm a huge *Hunger Games* fan, and thus I've written a story that has the characters of *RHPS* and *Shock Treatment* in the 'universe' and situations of the *Hunger Games* world… so I don't specifically write other fanfiction, but I do incorporate other fanfiction into *RHPS*. Not only is this fun, it helps keep the *RHPS* scene current in the eyes of fans new and old alike by crossing-over into new films and characters.

MCH: *Have you written any pieces that you're particularly proud of?*

BB: Yes, there is one piece I am especially proud of: 'ROCKY HORROR INFERNO'. It places one of the characters in *Rocky Horror*, Riff Raff, in the Hell of Dante's 'Inferno'. Riff plays Dante, a damned soul in hell, and Brad Majors (the hero of *Rocky Horror*) plays Virgil, who escorts him through Hell and eventual escape. I am proud of this one in particular because it was well received, and it was the first story that I had positive responses to before it was completed. A fan that read the first few chapters requested that I send her a complete copy as soon as possible, and that touched me. It's good to be appreciated.

MCH: *Jim, you recently urged Perry Bedden (who appeared in both* RHPS *and* Shock Treatment, *and played Riff Raff in the stage show at the King's Road Theatre and the West End Comedy Theatre production) to publish his never released behind the scenes photos of* RHPS *that resulted in Perry Bedden's Rocky Horror Picture Book (www.rockyhorrorpicturebook. com). Can you tell us a little about contributing to the project and what it has meant to you as a fan and to the fan community to have this new book available?*

JH: It meant the world to me. I bought some rare pictures from Perry a few years ago, not copies, I bought the masters! These still had tape on the back of them where he had taken them out of his scrapbook. And I scanned them and cleaned them up and mailed a copy back to him because I felt so bad taking them from him. He started posting some of them on Facebook. And I thought, you know what, between the two of us, we have quite a few of these, probably enough to do a book. I talked to some friends who helped me with it, Chris Holley and Dawn Marie. I had just left the show in Cincinnati that I had been doing for 20+ years and the project came along at just the right time. Perry mailed me a 90lb package of everything he had *Rocky Horror* wise. We found what we could use, scanned it, and put a book together. I've always been blessed with amazing resources. So we self-published the book and distributed it ourselves and it's been quite successful. It was the perfect project for me at the perfect time. Now it's out, and I am so proud of it. I think it may be the thing I am most proud of. Even over *Cosmo's Factory*.

MCH: *Are there any special books in your sizable* RHPS *collection?*

JH: Most fans have specific areas of collecting. Some collect audio, some collect photographs. Me, I collect books and advertising. I have quite a few things that I consider special for one reason or another, but if I had to pick one thing… I do have a signed copy of *Cosmic Light: The Birth of a Cult Classic* (1998). Jim Whitaker only printed a few hundred of those. They're pretty expensive on eBay now. I don't know of many of them out there, let alone signed. ●

Chapter
08

Sanity for Today: Brad and Janet's Post-Rocky Shock Treatment

Franck Boulègue

→ Jim Sharman's short (and promising) film career came to an abrupt end in 1981, six years after the release of *The Rocky Horror Picture Show*, with the critical and commercial failure of *Shock Treatment*, a musical/black comedy with many links to its predecessor. Highly underrated, the film can be read as a sort of a photographic negative of *Rocky*.

Figure 1: Denton's sanitized version of bliss © Twentieth Century Fox.

The microcosm it depicts – Denton and its inhabitants, all encompassed in a TV studio – represents the antithesis of the eccentric, transgressive and Dionysian community found in Frank-N-Furter's castle. If the two universes collided, Denton's conformism and conservatism would rapidly lead to the institutionalization of the 'Transylvanians' in its mental hospital and show: 'Dentonvale'.

From marriage maze to faith factory

Brad and Janet are back in this 'sequel/follow-up' to *RHPS* but, since they are played by different actors – Barry Botswick and Susan Sarandon in *Rocky*, Cliff De Young and Jessica Harper in *Shock Treatment* – we can wonder if they really are the same Brad and Janet. After all, 'Denton, USA' is basically 'Anytown, USA', and perhaps Brad and Janet are nothing more than 'the' typical American couple. They sit as members of the Denton TV audience for a show called 'Marriage Maze'. As in *Rocky*, the film begins with the traditional institution of heterosexual marriage, but attacks it from a different perspective this time. While the couple began their initial trip full of confidence, blessed by the church, here the strength of the link that unites them is questioned right away – though Judge Oliver Wright (a character who may or might not be the unnamed criminologist from *RHPS*) states:

Isn't that Brad and Janet Majors sitting in the audience, there? What an ideal couple. You know, more than anyone else in Denton, they represent the old values. Ike would have been proud of them.

Sanity for Today:
Brad and Janet's Post-Rocky Shock Treatment
Franck Boulègue

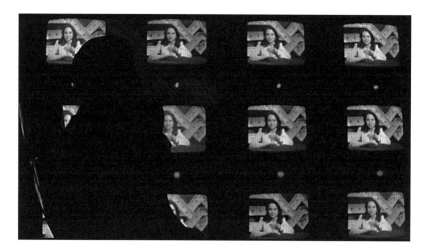

Figure 2: Janet's image is imprisoned by multiple screen
© Twentieth Century Fox.

Brad is labelled an 'emotional cripple' by the host of the show, a blind Austrian named Bert Schnick (reminiscent of Peter Sellers's *Dr. Strangelove* in the eponymous 1964 Stanley Kubrick film, or of Mike Myers's 'Dieter' from the 1980s *Saturday Night Live* sketch series *Sprockets* [NBC]). He convinces Janet and the audience that having Brad institutionalized in the 'Terminal Ward' of the local insane asylum – run by the incestuous siblings Dr Cosmo (Richard O'Brien) and Nation McKinley (Patricia Quinn), mirrors of Riff Raff and Magenta – is the best way to save their union. While Brad is left rotting behind bars, they rapidly transform Janet into 'Miss Mental Health'. She becomes the face of the 'Sanity for Today' Movement and is turned into a homemade rock-star by the leading team of Dentonvale. Later in the film, though, we find out that all this was really part of a secret plot designed by Farley Flavors (the owner of DTV and secret twin brother of Brad – a character prefiguring in some ways Pink's neo-fascist alter- ego in Alan Parker's *Pink Floyd – The Wall* [1982]) to seduce Janet and get revenge on his sibling. During his final 'Faith Factory' show, the truth is revealed and while Brad and Janet escape from the studio with several other dissenters of the new order (just as they escaped from Frank-N-Furter's castle before it was beamed back to Transylvania at the end of *Rocky*), Flavors sends the entire (and all too willing) audience to Dentonvale, while handing them striped straight-jackets.

From RKO to DTV

The process of reappropriation at work here is of a very interesting nature. While *RHPS* – as made clear in its opening song 'Science Fiction/Double Feature' – was composed of a patchwork of references to earlier horror and science fiction films – from *Doctor X* (Michael Curtiz, 1932) to *The Day of the Triffids* (Steve Sekely, 1962) – *Shock Treatment* recycles elements from the former and mirrors (and deforms) them through the televisual zeitgeist of the early 1980s. The two films thus form a diptych of sorts, an inverted pair. Eleven years later David Lynch's TV series, *On the Air* (ABC,1992), similarly recycled the 1950s – and Denton is in fact a very 'Lynchian' town, reminiscent of *Blue Velvet* (1986) for instance, in its depiction of superficial beauty that hides horrible secrets beneath its surface: 'You'll find a rambling rose, and a picket fence; tenderness and innocence, in Denton', sings one of Denton's residents in *Shock Treatment*.

If the two Sharman films were monsters, *The Rocky Horror Picture Show* would be (no surprise here) the creature of Dr Frankenstein, with its collage of cinematic transplants; *Shock Treatment*, on the other hand, would probably be best described as a doppelgänger, the omnipresent theme of the double permeating its very texture as a movie. As already mentioned above, many characters in *Shock Treatment* seem closely connected to their counterparts in *Rocky Horror*. The image of the McKinley siblings creates a clear visual and thematic reminder of their original Transylvanian equivalents (or are they really Riff Raff and Magenta come back to Earth for a different sort of experiment, less Gothic, more technological?). Ralph and Betty Hapschatt are also present. The central role of the twin brothers Brad and Farley, played by the same actor, is reminiscent of Patrick McGoohan's famous TV show *The Prisoner* (1967–1978), in which he was both the victim and the oppressor ('number 6' and 'number 1'). In *Shock Treatment*, Denton actually becomes a prison as inescapable as *The Prisoner*'s 'Village'. The duplication of the brothers underlines this unsettling ode to the mirror image. Consider the interchangeability of the members of the audience, as well as the walls of TV screens with similar images, which all contribute to the uncanny feeling generated by the focus on the notion of doubles.

Beyond *Shock Treatment*'s emphasis on the recycling of identical images, motifs and themes, many of which come from *RHPS*, several other allusions to *Rocky* are noteworthy. One of the most obvious is the presence of Frank-N-Furter's throne in 'Faith Factory', now painted red and occupied by a drugged and instrumentalized Janet. In the costume room of the studio we also briefly catch a glimpse of a reproduction of the famous *American Gothic* painting (1930) by Grant Wood, which was parodied during the opening of *RHPS*. Sal Piro, President of the Rocky Horror Picture Show Fan Club, also makes a brief cameo at the beginning of *Shock Treatment* as a man using a payphone.

While *RHPS* was about one cinema screen (from which many filmic references were extracted to create an alternate transgressive reality inside Frank-N-Furter's castle), *Shock Treatment* is, in an inverted but complimentary sort of way, really about many television screens (that swallow the world, providing conformist forms of entertainment).

Thank God, I'm a man!

To come back to the first song of *Rocky* and its celebration of naive cinematic science fiction from the 1930s to the 1950s, what really stands out is the fact that the audience's identification with the 'monsters' and 'aliens' (i.e. with Frank-N-Furter) of the film is, in many ways, much easier than it is with the supposedly human role-models who symbolize authority (Dr Everett Scott). This is especially true of the 'Red Scare' movies from the 1950s, referenced in the song 'Science Fiction/Double Feature', and their McCarthyst obsession with the total eradication of anything different (whether it has too many tentacles... or if it preaches something that sounds like Karl Marx's communist dogma).

This is very much the same feeling we have when confronted with the inhabitants of Denton: the impression of dealing with a group of potentially (but in a smiling sort

Sanity for Today:
Brad and Janet's Post-Rocky Shock Treatment
Franck Boulègue

of way) genocidal extremists. The connection is made clear in the film with the striped straight-jackets (reminiscent of the concentration-camp outfits from World War II, costume references that are also used in *RHPS*) handed to the audience by Farley Flavor, the local 'charismatic leader' (to speak like Max Weber, a sociologist who used this expression to characterize the hypnotic talents of politicians like Adolf Hitler).

In fact, during a commercial break for the 'Five Fs' or fast-food Farley Flavor ('Farley/Flavor/Fabulous/Fast/Food'), the logo, which appears, arranged in a circle, is highly reminiscent of a Nazi swastika. Bert even reveals his true ideological leanings close to the end of the film when he declares, speaking about Brad and Janet, 'They should be sent to the Danube at dawn!'. When asked to explain what he means by this, he simply answers: 'Just memories...'

The pink triangle that Frank-N-Furter was proudly wearing on his chest in *Rocky* comes in sharp contrast to the vision depicted here. No doubt Flavors would have asked him to go 'Out!' (of Denton and DTV) in no time, if their paths had crossed. The 'Out!' litany, started by Flavors and continued by the audience during 'Faith Factory', is of course a reminder of the 'Raus!' slogan of the Nazis, who meant to deport anyone out of the country who did not please their vision of racial purity. To quote Flavors: 'Sanity Today is the springboard to the hygienic tomorrow'.

What Flavors has created with DTV is a new version of the Absolutist State, with no separation between the TV stage and the rest of Denton. DTV, the omnipresent eye of its master, has swallowed up the universe around it. All the world's a (TV) stage, and the audience even sleeps in the studio, before being willingly deported to Dentonvale (which, by the way, is part of the studio too).

If *Rocky* was an ode to difference, individuality, transgression and love, *Shock Treatment* is a satire that illustrates just the opposite: it depicts a society in which brainless consumerism, conformism, pro-fascistic cleanliness ('help keep America clean' on the coffee stand), racism (though Denton claims its tolerance for the 'ethnic races', we later learn that Janet's father does not like Mexicans), hyper capitalism (advertisement pollutes everything), conservative ('always remember to follow the rules'), patriarchal and homophobic visions ('a man should call the toss, wear the pants and be the boss', 'faggots are maggots', 'Thank God I'm a man!') reign.

Sha(r)manism

It has unfortunately become a habit of sorts to describe both *RHPS* and *Shock Treatment* as nothing more than entertaining B-grade movies, without anything or very little to say about the world we live in, and without much exploration of their cinematography. It seems necessary, then, to re-evaluate the diptych these two films offer, and to stress the many levels of interpretation they facilitate, without forgetting the talent of all the participants involved in their creation.

First among them is Jim Sharman.

Contrary to the work of a director like Ed Wood – whose filmography has become the object of cult fandom because of its obvious (and often hilarious) lack of quality – the films of Sharman show nothing but extreme vitality. It is not his qualities as a director that are ridiculed by the shadow casts that perform in front of the movie screen, but the characters within the films. The films themselves are already making (good) fun of the shortcomings of the classics of science fiction and horror, which they recycle. The characters in *RHPS* and *Shock Treatment* are parodies already, archetypes that Sharman plays with.

It is impossible to mock the qualities of the film-making itself. More than professional, Sharman compares favourably with some of the masters of contemporary cinema. Regarding *Shock Treatment* (the same can be said for *Rocky*), one should notice the extremely well-designed camera movements that take place during complex sequences, reminiscent of the work of Brian De Palma (*Phantom of the Paradise*, 1974); the wonderful use of colours that permeate the screen in the style of Mario Bava and Dario Argento, or the immaculate white of the TV studio, not so different from what George Lucas did with his *THX 1138* (1971); and the moments when the characters sing while directly looking at the camera, reminiscent of early music videos with their choices of lighting (Janet singing 'In My Own Way', or in the song 'Me of Me', with its circling camera motion, pink lighting and 'live' music). If *RHPS* prefigured punk aesthetics, it could then be argued that *Shock Treatment* was among the precursors of the 1980s music video craze.

What is powerful, of course, is the fact that these filmic elements are perfectly integrated with the film's content. For instance, the cult of personality that characterizes music videos, with their overemphasis on the star's image, is shown here to rely on nothing less than the disintegration of the personality of the artists. Contrary to the fashion at work in Frank-N-Furter's castle, which is truly liberating in its transgressiveness and emphasis on individuality, Janet's 'little black dress' – a 'crowd pleaser' – is actually pretty conventional, beyond its MTV appeal.

Laugh/Applause

The relative lack of attention that Jim Sharman's filmography receives, despite a number of books and articles focused on *RHPS*, is worthy of consideration. One could argue that even the texts analysing *Rocky* do not really give enough credit to Sharman's talent and to the purely filmic elements of the production. While various publications explore

Sanity for Today:
Brad and Janet's Post-Rocky Shock Treatment
Franck Boulègue

RHPS as a collective experience, very little is available about the film itself. The fact that *The Rocky Horror Picture Show* is so much more than a movie – because it was origi-nally a stage show and lives on through its soundtrack, posters, audience participation and other fan phenomena – has led, paradoxically, to a certain under-appreciation of its filmic qualities. While many people discuss the experience of a *Rocky Horror* screen-ing, few write about its purely cinematic merits. In fact, the film-maker's name is rarely mentioned nor is the film examined in relationship to the rest of his career as a director.

Critics write a lot about audience participation as a means to explain the lasting suc-cess of the multimedia experience that *RHPS* has become, while they tend to describe the film itself as rather forgettable and plotless. Panned by the critics in 1975, and some-what overlooked as a work of art today beyond its participatory elements, the film as such appears greatly undervalued. However, Jim Sharman shows much talent in his film direction – a brio that becomes even more apparent when one watches his other works for the screen, all of them masterfully shot. *The Night The Prowler* (1978) is a fascinat-ing satire of Sydney's suburbs, seen through the eyes of a rebellious young woman, and *Shock Treatment* is in many ways as interesting as *RHPS*. One only wishes that his other two films – *Shirley Thompson vs. the Aliens* (1972) and *Summer of Secrets* (1976) – were more widely distributed.

Far from being a negligible moment in film history owing everything to the audience that appropriated it, *RHPS*'s cinematography is the work of a real artist – an artist who, much like Frank-N-Furter, sewed together a wonderful filmic creature that still wreaks havoc forty years after its birth. It is a monster which, though following the reactionary framework of the films it parodies and with its apparent final condemnation of its God-like mad scientist, transcends the explicit content of its message to transmit a latent celebration of the liberation of social norms and filmic rules – a recurrent message in the cinema of Sharman.

For too long the focus has solely remained on intertextuality and audience participa-tion. This is likely due to the collective nature of *Rocky Horror*'s famous screenings that have eclipsed any other aspects of the film. The fact that we seem to be moving away from the era when most 'virgins' view the film for the first time in a movie theatre and more towards home cinema and DVDs, might actually be the best thing possible for the film itself – though probably not for the collective experience, of course. It is now pos-sible to reassess the film's intrinsic cinematic virtues, away from the chaos that usually surrounds its movie screenings. This re-evaluation of the film itself might help us bet-ter understand the real cinematic know-how developed by Sharman married to Richard O'Brien's brilliant creation, without which, *Rocky Horror*'s ensuing cult phenomena might not have been possible. Contrary to popular explanation, the film's cult status is anything but 'accidental' in that its lasting impact can be, at least in part, credited to Sharman's talent. If *RHPS* had simply been a bad film that people jokingly yelled at, the phenomenon likely would have been little more than a short-lived attraction.

In this general process of reassessment, watching and analysing the other films of Sharman – beginning with *Shock Treatment* – outside live screenings, might be an interesting way to re-evaluate the filmic qualities of *RHPS* and its director's filmography.

Quiet

As with *RHPS*, *Shock Treatment* has generated a process of reappropriation by various film audiences around the globe, albeit to a lesser extent through shadow casts that perform the film in front of movie screens. Nevertheless, the success of such interactive experiences remains rather anecdotal when compared to the ongoing success of *Rocky*. How can this be explained?

Part of the answer might be found in the fact that the film already has an audience of its own, the people of Denton, who constantly talk back to the characters onstage following cues (such as the 'Laugh Applause Quiet' sign) fed to them by the programmers of DTV. There is not much room for a second shadow cast to infiltrate this already interactive process occurring in the film.

Moreover, one might wonder who would want to 'dress up' as the people from Denton. Their fashion choices are supposed to represent a very boring and conservative American way of life, away from the outrageousness of the style favoured by Frank-N-Furter and his followers. What makes *RHPS* so much fun is partly linked to the transgressive nature of the way one can dress at screenings. If that aspect of the game were to be removed, and if additionally it became more difficult to talk back to the screen due to a second audience's interference, it is likely that the *Rocky* phenomenon would not be what it has become.

Today although *Shock Treatment* benefits from its own fan club and tributes, the film was poorly distributed until recently and remains in the shadow of its predecessor. Its initial failure at the box office can partly be explained by the context in which it was released. As is evident with *RHPS*'s broadcast of Nixon's resignation speech during Brad and Janet's rainy car ride, the film was released following a political event that shook the very certainties of the United States, enabling the rise of a transgressive culture that would have had difficulties surfacing on such a scale in any previous generation. On the other hand, *Shock Treatment* was shot and released at a moment in American history when the country was on its way to electing a very conservative president, Ronald Reagan's 'revolution'. The 40th President of the United States – and former Hollywood ac-

Sanity for Today:
Brad and Janet's Post-Rocky Shock Treatment
Franck Boulègue

tor – was about to return political debate to topics focused on family values and prayer in schools, moving away from the various progressive policies of the previous twenty years towards a country ruled by TV shows like *Dallas* (David Jacobs, CBS, 1978–91) and *Dynasty* (Esther and Richard Shapiro, ABC, 1981–89).

It is possible that the visionary and darker aspects of *Shock Treatment* were detrimental to its success in this context. Sharman and O'Brien were great satirists and the final statement of the film is nothing less than bleak. The totalitarian society it depicts – which can be described as a prison State – behind all the songs, bright colours and shiny teeth – probably felt too close to reality in many ways for the film to succeed: Welcome to Denton: The Home of Happiness! ●

GO FURTHER

Online

'Shock Treatment: Introduction by Sal Piro'
Sal Piro
RockyHorror.org (n.d.), http://www.rockyhorror.com/shocktreatment/introduction.php.

Website

'Shock Treatment Links': http://www.theshocktreatmentnetwork.com/links.htm

'IT'S A WEEKLY FAMILY GATHERING. THERE ARE LIFELONG BONDS THAT CAME ABOUT AND CONTINUE TO COME ABOUT BECAUSE THIS FILM IS STILL PLAYING IN THEATRES.'

LARRY VIEZEL

Chapter
09

'Don't Dream It, Be It': The Method in the Madness of *The Rocky Horror Picture Show*

Sarah Cleary

→ I'd never been to a live *Rocky Horror* before, nor had I seen the film, so when it came to a costume, I hadn't a clue what to wear. Once I got into the Sugar Club, [where the screenings took place], I couldn't believe it. People were dressed in next to nothing! In all sorts of outfits from the film. Some [costumes] were just crazy.

Figure 1: Contrary to typical readings of The Rocky Horror Picture Show audience members use the screening as a platform to wear the most outrageous costumes, which often have little if anything to do with the show © Hector Heathwood Photography.

After about twenty minutes into the film, I realised that people watching and participating in the show didn't care what people had on them, or whether their legs were too fat or too thin or scarred like mine. Everyone was just so happy to be there. It was then that I decided. I told my friend I was going to the loo and while there I slipped off my jeans, tucked them into my bag. The majority of people there weren't wearing pants; so why should I? Even though I had on a pair of plain cotton knickers and my beat up Dr Martin's boots, it felt great to be part of the show.

The above statement is taken from a fan whom I interviewed a number of years ago when I first started producing the Rocky Horror Picture Show Ireland. It has not only remained an inspiration to continue *The Rocky Horror Picture Show*, but it also has become the motivation behind this chapter. Informed by a decade's worth of *RHPS* live performances, I will undertake a fresh analysis of the participatory element of the *RHPS* audience, with a view to expanding traditional concepts of fandom into a more transgressive reading of the spectator as actor, distilled from readings that consider the alleged implications of conformity through ritual and repetition.

In doing so, the aim of the chapter is to provide a conceptual framework based on the premise of 'participation as active performance'. Moreover drawing on the work of Russian actor and director Constantin Stanislavski and others, this chapter will address the theatricality of the *RHPS* experience and recognize its fans as 'Method' actors, simultaneously creating and performing on a liminal stage, defined by the contours of their own experience and imagination. The acting technique known as Method, stems from a system of acting techniques that Stanislavski developed at the Moscow Art Theatre with the playwright and author Anton Chekhov. In *Method Acting Reconsidered* (2000), David Krasner remarks how Method, 'is an acting technique that stresses truthful behaviour in imaginary circumstances. It trains the actor to make demands on the body through the use of stimuli and imagination, so that the body responds creatively'. Expanding upon Stanislavski's term *perezhivanie* (often translated as 'a lived experience'), he follows that the Method actor creates an organic and imaginative performance by experiencing or 'living through' the role. It is my contention that the actions of an audience immersed

'Don't Dream It, Be It':
The Method in the Madness of *The Rocky Horror Picture Show*
Sarah Cleary

in the participation of an *RHPS* live event are similarly founded on an analogous (though obviously not identical) model of 'organic acting'.

Figure 2: Audience members throwing themselves into the show © Hector Heathwood Photography.

Audience reception and participation at *RHPS* is a popular subject covered in great depth throughout film and media studies. However, research over the years has, recurrently, sought to drive a wedge between the screening and the performance of the audience. Second, the generalizability of many of the publications on this issue is problematic as it overlooks the individual motivations of audience members. Furthermore, because of the reoccurring nature of the event, *RHPS* is considered in danger of diminishing its more transgressive qualities through repetition and ritual.

Introducing the work of Barry E. Grant, Ernest Mathijs and Jamie Sexton in *Cult Cinema* (2007) observe how complications to the *RHPS* live experience, lie in the fact that 'it can be performed, faked'. Accordingly, in his article 'Science Fiction Double Feature', Grant associates a lack of realism with the seemingly over-performed and contrived nature of audience participation:

> [T]he predetermined costumes, repetition of the character's lines at specific times, and the ritualization of certain acts during the screening (throwing rice or toilet paper) ultimately reconstitutes *outside* the film a community not unlike the one lampooned *within* it. The role quality of these rituals, which discourage the spontaneous improvisation by newcomers, suggests that the community is in its own way every bit as conformist and repressive as the middle class satirized on the screen.

Yet, in direct opposition to such a claim, in his introduction to *The Official Audience Par-tic-i-pation Guide* (2006), *RHPS* pioneer Sal Piro warns audience members of making fun of somebody not in the *exact* attire, thus undermining Grant's reductionist view of *RHPS*. In addition to this warning, Piro counsels how, 'The point is that their heart is in it and this might discourage them or others from ever returning in costumes and that's what this cult's all about'.

Seen from another perspective, in *Reading Rocky Horror: The Rocky Horror Picture Show and Popular Culture* (2008), Jeffery Weinstock points out how the perceptible environment in which the audience inhabits prevents 'imaginary identification with the filmic text'. Getting hit with rice for Weinstock, jerks spectators back into reality, disrupting the pretence they have established with costuming and call backs. Expanding upon this notion, Weinstock asserts that:

> What the audience's simultaneous empathetic actions materialize is the inchoate and unarticulated desire on the part of the audience of the classic plot-driven film to be absorbed into the film, to be a part of the experience to such an extent that

Figure 3: Shadow cast
member of the Rocky
Horror Picture Show Ireland
© Hector Heathwood
Photography.

boundaries between the narrative world and the real-life world of the audience dissolve. However, dance movements and the use of props 'rematerialize' the viewing experience, ground the viewer in the bodily experience of spectatorship, and thereby disrupt psychic identification.

Unlike Patrick Kinkade and Michael Katovich who, in their article 'Toward a Sociology of Cult Films: Reading "Rocky Horror"' (1992), observe how the film endorses 'narcissistic and empathic identification with subversive characters', Weinstock argues that this form of identification, when accessible, is problematic as it suggests audience interaction as some form of sacred practice. A major weakness of such an analysis, according to Weinstock, is that it leaves little room for the ironic interplay of audience interjections throughout the screening that essentially 'interrupt the narrative in ways that prevent absorption or identification'. He does nonetheless, acknowledge that the audience's investment in the cult film with the characters on the screen is based on a form of 'love' that embraces what J. P. Telotte defines a 'comfortable difference'. However, because this love springs from an ironic sensibility, it is essentially a sadist form of love that 'continually insults and degrades the objects of its affection'.

While only scratching the surface of 'audience participation' in film theory, what is clear from these assessments of the cult phenomena is that there exists a number of tensions between spectacle and spectator. On the one hand as Grant advocates, the film imposes itself upon audiences, reminding them, that no matter how much they participate in the real world, the fictionality of RHPS will always exert dominance. On the other hand, views such as the one Weinstock upholds, proposes a dynamic whereby the audience is constantly trying to impose itself upon the film, through the use of what he calls 'interjections' that constantly seek to disrupt the linear narrative of the film.

In an effort to ease such tensions, Heather C. Levy and Matthew A. Levy in their Reading Rocky Horror article, 'Mocking the Mirror', employ the philosopher Jean Baudrillard's concept of hyperreality; a concept which seeks to describe the inability to distinguish a real object or event from that of a simulation or copy. Observing that traditional concepts of film spectatorship flounder in the presence of an RHPS audience, they write how 'Audience participation at the Rocky Horror reveals a falsifying opposition between viewers and viewed that continues to vex psychoanalytic models of film spectatorship'. In contrast, Baudrillard's model of simulated reality serves as a useful framework through which the motivations for RHPS audience participation are viewed

'Don't Dream It, Be It':
The Method in the Madness of *The Rocky Horror Picture Show*
Sarah Cleary

in isolation from the typical 'subject–object binary' of spectator and spectacle. Indulging their passion for the show, '*Rocky Horror* spectators see that their world is fake and decide to have fun with it rather than to despair or act desperately to make things authentic again'. Though such an analysis establishes a fresh mode of approaching audience spectatorship, there is a slight tendency to deviate from the sphere of theatricality which foregrounds the *RHPS* experience.

Ebbing closer to such a theatrical analysis, in 'Semiotics by Instinct', another article in *Reading Rocky Horror*, Ann Jerslev, not only highlights the role of spectator as actor, but seeks to create a tone within her analysis of *RHPS* whereby spectator and film are not in a constant battle for supremacy. She argues that:

> the heart of the matter in […] cult culture is the deconstruction (either obvious or less obvious, but always playful) of the film text's position of superiority; of the text unfolding itself in front of the reader, thus placing and constructing a position of reading for the spectator. This deconstructive discourse is called 'radical bricolage' by Corrigan (1986). The textual discourse is put into play by means of the spectators pretending to be directors of and actors in the film at the same time. The cult events may be understood at the same time as a construction of and as travelling through a fictional universe.

Similar to the views suggested here, Jerslev advocates an approach whereby the investigation into the 'clash' between the audience and the cult film is of more importance than further frustrating opposing binary concepts. Ascribing the term 'cult event' to the 'signifying practice' of this clash, she writes how:

> I find this particular clash interesting for two reasons, both as a cultural practice and as a sort of textual staging. In the first place, it may be read as signifying postmodern culture in a wider sense. I use the concept postmodern here merely to indicate a mode of comprehension that transgresses modernity's hierarchized construction of meaning: the cult event speaks of cultural practice that invalidates already fixed cultural codes, and constructs a certain relation between the filmic texts and their audiences on grounds of a perceptual cognition structured as an intertextual encyclopaedia.

Nevertheless, as Mathijs and Mendik note in their introduction to Jerslev's article, she prioritizes the cognitive nature of the audience over that of the performative. Moreover, a key problem with any analysis of *RHPS* is how the actual text, in juxtaposition with the participation of the live audience, should be read. On the one hand it is fundamentally a transgressive production that dissolves gender roles and inverts traditional assumptions about sexuality. On the other, it could be read as an essentially heteronormative

Figure 4: Audience members
© Hector Heathwood
Photography.

and conformist text, whereby the apparent stringency of the rituals ultimately, as Grant claims, 'redeem[s] that which they seem to violate'. In the end, what is lost in such a binary opposition is the individual reception of the participant and their assimilation of the experience. Therefore in an effort to reconcile this binary opposition between subject and object, I now propose a reading of the *RHPS* audience as actors, hopefully reconciling many of the issues highlighted earlier in the chapter.

As previously mentioned, throughout critical theory on *RHPS*, there exists a strong tendency as Mathijs and Sexton note to posit 'ritualized audience response' and 'predetermined costumes and repetition of character lines', as a sign of how any 'transgression the film might have carried over onto viewers was now undone'. Similarly, when all is said and done, complimenting various eccentricities informing the unconventionality of the *RHPS*, 'the question remains whether multiple layers of performativity do not make it unnecessarily difficult for audiences to access any liberatory content that might lead to personal liberation'.

In order to overcome such concerns, the notion of performance must be altered to include a system, which not only seeks to incorporate both audience participation in conjunction with the established text, but allows room for the individual to experience the transgressive qualities of the show's narrative effectively time and time again. Thus hijacking the cinematic space in favour of the theatrical realm, which by its live nature is a more fluid medium, is a much more beneficial endeavour.

Total immersion of mind and body, is often hampered for the audience during a typical performance, by the very restrictions of the stage, the limitations of props and the mundane necessity of theatrical cues such as lighting and curtain calls. However, a reading such as the one I propose, reveals no such limits as the performance becomes embedded within the audience, reflecting a meta-reality which facilitates a co-dependence between the audience and the screen. At the root of this co-dependence is not necessarily a submission on the part of the spectator to go along with whatever happens, but his or her active participation within a 'role', thus using the entirety of the theatre as an extension of the stage.

While its origins are of course steeped in theatre, the cult of *RHPS* participation emerged at a time when live theatre underwent a process of change and experimentation, whereby traditional conventions were inverted and the use of audience participation was explored as an innovative dramaturgical device. As a play first and foremost, which has essentially returned to the theatre, *RHPS* straddles multiple mediums with varying degrees of force. First, at a *RHPS* live event the film is screened for its audience. What sets the show apart from a typical screening is the shadow cast miming in sync with the film, bringing to life the characters within daring proximity of the audience. Consequently, for the most part, this has the effect of obliterating the 'fourth wall'

'Don't Dream It, Be It':
The Method in the Madness of *The Rocky Horror Picture Show*
Sarah Cleary

Figure 5: Anything Goes: Audience members © Hector Heathwood Photography.

which in most other productions, typically confines the audience, while firmly establishing boundaries between stage and audience.

Conversely, *RHPS* has no such boundaries and welcomes the merger between actor and audience; spectator and spectacle. As a play which has no clear demarcations as to where the audience starts and the actors begin, the shadow cast players on the stage are completely aware of the inevitability of being hit with toast or having their choreography disrupted and solemnity tested as the audience's hijinks often leaves one turning away to laugh quite unprofessionally into the shoulder of a fellow shadow actor. Contrarily, the 'audience as actors', fulfils a much more intense and pure role than the authorized cast on the formal stage. The entire performance of the audience as a whole, not just the proceedings on the stage, is part of this imaginative narrative, which for that evening is as authentic as the individuals making up the audience will it. Emboldened by the established narrative of the film, the *RHPS* fan takes on a role of their own making. This may not necessarily always be an emulation of an *RHPS* character. Very often audience members will don the most outrageous of costumes, which have nothing to do with the show, simply because within the imaginative realms of 'Transsexual Transylvania' anything goes.

Similarly, as Richard Hahlo and Peter Reynolds note of the theatrical workshop in *Dramatic Events* (2000), when it comes to audience participation, there must be a certain desire on the part of the individual to act in a dangerous manner that contradicts his or her usual disposition.

> Those taking part, especially if it is a new experience for them, have to be encouraged to get to a point where they can begin to take small but significant personal risks, and prick the bubble of inhabiting self-consciousness. The workshop leader [...] won't physically or even metaphorically have to drag spectators into active participation, but she or he will inevitably gently need to persuade and cajole sometimes reluctant spectators into positions where they become active participants in making a dramatic event of their own.

It is my contention, that for the individual who is willing, the *RHPS* live experience acts as a form of enticing and encouraging *cicerone* or theatrical chaperon. Props, costumes and call backs help with this gentle cajoling, allowing the spectator, as Hahlo and Reynolds observe, to maintain their own dramatic event, facilitated through a form of 'organic acting'. Moreover, the fact that it is a communal activity where the 'stage' is shared by a theatrical space full of people allows individuals to push personal boundaries. In essence, as long as everybody in the room is dressed completely outrageously exclaiming lewd remarks, placates, or at least goes a long way towards appeasing, the insecurities inherent within the group, as evidenced by my introductory excerpt.

Figure 6: Shadow cast
members of the Rocky Horror
Picture Show Ireland © Hector Heathwood Photography.

The audience, when willing, is 'transported to another world' whereby meanings and the order of everyday life is inverted and transgressed in a manner which is unique to that individual. For some it is the inversion of gender through dress, of sexuality through exhibitionism and for others it's simply wearing silly hats and shouting 'slut' and 'asshole' at random strangers. Ultimately, for most, this transportation is made possible through total immersion into their 'role'.

The *RHPS* ability, as Robert E. Wood astutely notes, 'to generate an audience *for* its audience', is *the* key feature of the show. From this it is possible to construe the typical cinematic gaze as inverted and looking *out* upon the spectacle of the audience as actors. While still fully aware of their role as a fictional character, audience members use their surroundings, their props and ultimately each other to enforce a suspension of disbelief until the credits role. Correspondingly, as David Z. Saltz astutely notes of Stanislavski's conceptions of 'organic', in 'The Reality of Doing: Real Speech Acts in the Theatre' (2000), such acting 'transforms whatever social reality the actors choose to portray into a living reality, at least for the duration of the performance event'. For the *RHPS* audience member, there is no pretence, just a pure form of immersive and highly mutable role play, far removed from the strict ritualized format certain critics espouse. In his seminal book *A Dream of Passion* (1988), the father of Method in America, Lee Strasberg, similarly found that 'Method considers the actor as a creative artist who must translate the ideas, intentions, and words of the author into living presentation'. Through the perpetual movement and transformation of the audience, *RHPS* is constantly in motion, hence the root of its transgressive nature.

Expanding on this last point, it is arguable that a particular ethos and philosophy was forever distilled in the print of the 1975 film. Nonetheless, through the use of audience participation, especially when read through the context of a Method framework, Richard O'Brien's characters, which may have forever been locked within an immutable form, are given a fresh lease of life each show, through the performances of thousands of their fans as they role play. At the start of each show an entire new cast is born as a product of the collective imagination of the audience, and similarly, by the end of the night, this particular and unique dynamic meets its demise. Thus the communal imaginative space of *RHPS* engenders immersive roles which audience members can, if they so wish, indulge to their heart's content. After nearly fifty live shows as both producer and 'Janet', I cannot say that I have experienced the same show twice, which is why the performative actions of the *RHPS* audience must be interpreted with caution, as moving too far from its theatrical roots merely obscures the role of audience as actors, a point which Saltz is careful to highlight:

Theatrical models that drive a wedge between performance and reality, such as semiotics […] suppress the radically transformative potential of theatrical perfor-

'Don't Dream It, Be It':
The Method in the Madness of *The Rocky Horror Picture Show*
Sarah Cleary

mance. They deny theatre its ability to explore and expose – and not merely to assert or signify – the nature of the games that structure our own lives and to demonstrate ways we might change the rules.

By way of conclusion, I return to yet another Irish *Rocky* fan who, having embodied the spirit of audience as actor, professed how:

[t]he atmosphere when you go to the show is simply amazing. Though everyone is dressed up, nobody is hiding anything. You can be free to just go crazy and nobody will bat an eyelid, they'll actually jump right into the madness with you! There are so few events where males in particular can dress up in a corset and suspenders and be embraced rather than be received with raised eyebrows. There just isn't that fear of rejection based on what you're wearing, anyone there can become your greatest friend!

As Lawrence O'Toole observes, *RHPS* is capable of sending 'its audiences into paroxysms of joy, allowing them to disport their own personal fantasies in the theatre'. As a result of such pure indulgence, the *Rocky* audience isn't faking, why would they? Nor, from the point of view of this producer, are they taking part in a formal ritual. Instead they are performers, playing a part while acting out these personal fantasies. Not dreaming *it*. But being *it*. ●

GO FURTHER

Books

The Cult Reader
Ernest Mathijs and Xavier Mendik (eds)
(Berkshire: Open University Press, 2008)

The Mouse Machine: Disney and Technology
J. P. Telotte
(Illinois: UIP, 2008)

Cult Cinema: An Introduction
Ernest Mathijs and Jamie Sexton
(West Sussex: John Wiley & Sons, 2007)

The Official Audience Par-tic-i-pation Guide
Sal Piro
(London: Harper Collins, 2006)

Dramatic Events: How to Run a Successful Workshop
Peter Reynolds and Richard Hahlo
(London: Faber & Faber Limited, 2000)

Method Acting Reconsidered: Theory, Practice, Future
David Krasner (ed.)
(New York: St Martin's Press, 2000)

Simulacra and Simulation
Jean Baudrillard
(Ann Arbor: University of Michigan Press, 1994)

A Dream of Passion: The Development of the Method
Lee Strasberg
(London: Penguin, 1988)

An Actor Prepares
Constantin Stanislavski
(London: Eyre Methuen, 1980)

Essays/Extracts/Articles

'Toward a Sociology of Cult Films: Reading "Rocky Horror"'
Patrick T. Kinkade and Michael A. Katovich
In *The Sociological Quarterly*. 33 (1992), pp. 191–208.

Fan Appreciation no. 6
Larry Viezel, Collector Extraordinaire

Interviewed by Marisa C. Hayes

Marisa C. Hayes (MCH): *Tell us a little about your* RHPS *collection: how many items do you own and what are some of your most rare or prized pieces?*

Larry Viezel (LV): I started collecting in (I think) 1994 in college. There was a man at the campus centre who sold posters. I picked up a giant poster of Kurt Cobain and some 8 × 10 stills from *Rocky Horror*. I remember thinking about how I wanted to collect all of the photos from 'The Denton Affair' (the book that the narrator uses in the film). Shortly thereafter I went to a comic book store downtown and found a copy of *Weird Fantasy* #13 – the comic book used in 'The Denton Affair'. And it was all down hill from there. I started collecting everything I could get my hands on – specifically photos. There were a TON of photos taken on the set. There were two main on-set photographers, Mick Rock, the famous glam-rock photographer who photographed such iconic images as the Queen album cover, and John Jay, who was the still photographer for movies like *Star Wars* (1977) and *2001: A Space Odyssey* (1968). There were also personal photographs taken on the set by actors and crew members. I have over 1,000 on-set photos between the two photographers.

Some prized pieces in my collection include:

- A collection of behind-the-scenes photographs originally from the studio's archives. An intern at Twentieth Century Fox was tasked with cleaning out a flooded storeroom in the early 1980s. While much of what was in there was ruined, he saved some of the less damaged goods. This included lots and lots of pictures and slides from classic movies in the 1970s. Because of that, I now have over 300 behind-the-scenes *Rocky Horror* photos in my collection. I can't imagine that these would have been lost to the ages were it not for this guy!
- Original costume pieces – Little Nell's sequined bustier worn from the 'Time Warp' dance number through the first half of the movie. One of the organza boas used in the floorshow. Rings and cufflinks worn by the Transylvanians. I got the bustier and boa from Sue Blane's costume assistant, Yasmin Pettigrew. After the movie wrapped, she wound up with the bulk of the costumes. She would often let neighbourhood kids play with them and several of them disappeared over the years. But these two she saved.
- A Japanese press book signed by nine of the ten main actors in the movie as well as many extras and members of the crew. I hope to get Peter Hinwood's autograph next time I travel to London.

Fan Appreciation no. 6
Larry Viezel

- Over 100 posters from the film. Most of these are stored in tubes, but I have some hung up, including a 40 × 60 'legs' poster. There are fewer than a dozen of these known to collectors.
- Original costume sketches by costume designer Sue Blane. I have two original pieces – one from the wedding scene in the movie and one of Riff Raff and Eddie from the original play. I also have a bunch of negatives from when she photographed them for use in *The Rocky Horror Scrapbook* [1998].
- Original handwritten lyrics of the opening song 'Science Fiction/ Double Feature' by author Richard O'Brien (including some notes he was scrawling about the 'I Can Make You a Man' song from the show on the back of the page).
- All of producer Michael White's personal notes regarding *Rocky Horror* – including original scripts, a proposed but never released script for a sequel, actors contracts (including Tim Curry, Susan Sarandon, Barry Bostwick, Meatloaf and Richard O'Brien), letters and correspondence. Getting my hands on this was like finding The Lost Ark of the Covenant of *Rocky Horror* memorabilia.

I also have albums, posters, trading cards, books, DVDs, VHSs, calendars, toys and dolls. It's a pretty exhaustive collection. People used to joke that if someone wrote 'Rocky Horror' on a napkin I'd be by with an offer in not too long. I don't think that's quite true, but it made me smile. There are a few things that 'got away' over the years and my collecting has slowed down considerably since I have had my daughter. But I still love each and every piece. It's funny, sometimes I forget what I have. I love going 'spelunking' through it to see what I can find.

I really do love Etsy and the spirit of creating new art. Beyond Etsy I also recommend sites like *RedBubble* for some really inventive *Rocky Horror* mashup T-shirts. I love the Disney-style logo featuring Oakley Court (the castle from the movie) and the words 'Rocky Horror' in the classic Mickey signature font. I recently started collecting original *Rocky Horror*-themed art pieces. A few of the pieces I own are by members of the *Rocky Horror* performing community. Michael 'Epyon5' Jones has done some wonderful work as has Katrina Catizone and Karly Dytrych. We commissioned a deck of cards from Karly for the 2008 Rocky Horror Convention and I have the original artwork used for the jokers sitting above my desk.

MCH: *You own the* RockyHorror.org *domain name, how has RHPS fan-*

dom evolved with the digital age? For example, I see lots of memes float-
ing around online that continue the tradition of creating word play and
interactive dialogue with Rocky's story and characters. There are also
costume tutorials, forums, and screening listings, etc. What do you enjoy
most about virtual fandom?

LV: The rise of the Internet significantly changed *Rocky Horror* fandom.
I got in just as the web really started to take off. It used to be that if you
wanted to interact with like-minded weirdos you had to stumble upon a
local weekly showing of *Rocky Horror*. Every show was a melting pot of all
different outcasts: band geeks, science fiction fans, theatre nerds, comic
book geeks, gays, punks, burnouts – if you didn't fit in, there was a home
for you at *Rocky Horror*. It was a safe haven for everyone who ever felt
they had nowhere to fit in. And it still is that way today – the home hasn't
gone away. But now there are homes for each one of these types of outcasts right in the comfort of their own living room or closer, in their own
pockets. The Internet has given us an infinite amount of forums to meet
specifically like-minded individuals.

eBay changed collecting quite a bit. There was a time when certain
collectibles were so rare that they would command quite a hefty price
tag. But eBay made it a lot easier to sell things, so the market got flooded.
On the other hand, eBay has led me to some great finds. I wouldn't have
half the impressive stuff in my collection without it.

I should mention two other great things that came about for *Rocky
Horror* online. The first is YouTube. Fan videos have really taken off on
YouTube. Some of them are really hilarious. There is one, titled 'Backwards Cactus' that features Weird Al's 'Bohemian Rhapsody' set to *Rocky
Horror*, but in reverse. It's very amusing how well it fits. Another was an
amateur video called 'Rocky Horror in 30 Minutes'. It's a very very low-
budget version of the show, deleting some characters (Eddie) entirely.
It looks as if it was put together by a 13 year old with his family pitching
in to perform the roles in the show. The end result is hysterical. You can
tell that the director's intentions came from an honest pure love of the
source material, but was clearly limited by resources and capabilities. Another favourite is Sins O' The Flesh's 'The Drunky Horror Picture Show'.
The whole show is told – very crassly, out of order and quite bizarrely – by a
man who has had wayyyy too much alcohol to be coherent. Beyond comedy videos, there are also some amazingly professionally put together
videos that show you the quality of the work put out by this community.
Of particular note are The Home of Happiness videos 'Shots', 'Tonight's

Gonna Be a Good Night', 'Give Me Everything' and 'Selfie'. I'll give you the links to all of these. Give them a whirl.

"Backwards Cactus" – http://youtu.be/t-l8Vlr_mF8
"Rocky Horror in 30 Minutes" – http://bit.ly/Z9l8rw
"Drunky Horror" – http://youtu.be/g7WwOOuwSIM
"Shots" – http://youtu.be/C6ME-gkkAfA
"Tonight" – http://youtu.be/81FXOp3mslU
"Give Me Everything" – http://youtu.be/X40bOHDaPts
"Selfie" – http://youtu.be/gpSvJ-gB--s

And finally, crowd-funding. This past year we leveraged crowd-funding to produce the *Rocky Horror Saved My Life* documentary. It was amazing to see the entire community come together and donate to support making this project come to fruition. The end result is going to be fantastic. ●

*Larry Viezel with his
collection © Kate Viezel.*

Chapter
10

Mercy Killing: Rocky Horror, the Loss of Innocence and the Death of Nostalgia

Andrew Howe

→ **While seeming to celebrate the 1930s, 1940s and 1950s with its witty homages to the popular cinema and music of the time, *The Rocky Horror Picture Show* takes a pickaxe to certain aspects of traditional western culture. First and foremost are the film's frank assertions regarding the manufactured nature of traditional heterosexuality.**

Fresh off of their engagement, Brad and Janet are quickly drawn into the alternative lifestyle of Dr Frank-N-Furter, whose sexual machinations are comically sanctioned due to his status as a 'scientist'. The message is clear: humans are sexual creatures, and Alfred Kinsey and his ilk merely vocalized what everyone already knew but were afraid to openly discuss. Frank's easy temptations of both members of this red-blooded couple are indicative of the changes brought by the sexual revolution in the United States and Western Europe. Janet's seduction suggests something about the decline of serial monogamy in the 1960s, Brad's about the rising visibility of homosexuality. The death of Eddie is also symbolic of the decline of an era, as Frank, with his glitzy, David Bowie-inspired glam look *literally* kills the more traditional rock-and-roll singer. Accused of excess by his minions Riff Raff and Magenta, Frank is slated for destruction. In a last ditch effort to save himself, he vocalizes the spirit of nostalgia against which he has been crusading for the entire narrative, via the song 'I'm Going Home'. The lyric 'Cause I've seen blue skies through the tears in my eyes / And I realize, I'm going home' advances the idea that backward motion is possible, that previously vacated, even repudiated identities can be re-occupied, despite the loss of innocence. However, it is too late for Frank-N-Furter, and it is too late for society. Following the assassination of Martin Luther King Jr and the Manson murders in the United States, and Bloody Sunday in the United Kingdom, as well as a number of other extreme events that marked the late 1960s and early 1970s, the quaint vision of a traditional and moral society was gone forever. As the film was a product of both British theatre and the Hollywood film industry, this chapter situates this loss of innocence, and the narrative unease regarding the competing projects of hedonism and nostalgia that follow, as a cross-Atlantic affair.

Although in many ways it is a film that looks backwards while simultaneously pondering the future, *The Rocky Horror Picture Show* roots itself to a specific time and place: 8 August 1974, in Denton, Ohio. The film was created during a period of political and, in particular, economic upheaval in both of its source nations. By August 1975 and the film's release, the United States had suffered humiliating setbacks in their foreign policy (the loss of the Vietnam War), their politics (the resignation of President Richard Nixon due to the burgeoning Watergate scandal) and their economy (the failure of the Bretton Woods monetary system, which made the dollar a flat currency). The British had also experienced a series of embarrassing defeats, including the London Gold Pool Collapse, the rationing of electricity in the Three Day Week crisis, and the near complete loss of imperial and even regional influence, symbolized first by the loss of the Suez Canal and later the inability to protect traditional fishing waters in the North Atlantic during the three so-called 'Cod Wars' with Iceland. Both nations suffered from high unemployment, expensive oil due to the 1973 Oil Crisis, stagnant economies and rampant inflation. Setting the film on the evening of 8 August 1974, concurrent with the resignation speech of President Richard Nixon, situates the events of the narrative within a greater contextual malaise. Much as Brad and Janet are slated to lose their personal in-

Mercy Killing: Rocky Horror, the Loss of Innocence and the Death of Nostalgia
Andrew Howe

nocence due to the designs of Frank-N-Furter, so too had these two nations lost the optimism and upward trajectory that typified the early years of the post-World War II period. By the mid-1970s, neither the United States nor England had fulfilled the goals they had once believed they could, and had been brought low by a variety of factors.

Figure 1: Brad courts Janet in front of a billboard promoting Denton © Twentieth Century Fox.

The film thus mirrors the unsettled nature of the times in which it was produced while simultaneously reflecting anxieties involving rites of passage that cut across generational lines. According to Richard O'Brien – in Dave Thompson's *Music on Film* (2012) – it is this latter dimension that has driven its continued popularity:

> Inside this tale, we're talking about puberty and the journey from childhood into adulthood. *Rocky*'s exactly like that. A rite of passage. A journey. Brad and Janet are basically Hansel and Gretel, and Frank-N-Furter is the wicked witch. That's its true longevity. It's not just pantomime and nonsense; it has this unspoken depth which makes it deeply appealing.

Although it was released during a time of turmoil, the film is such that it can be enjoyed by generation after generation, as it also resonates with the turmoil that attends the passage through adolescence. The film was thus culturally resonant to two western powers, the citizens of whom had lost their innocence either in the jungles of Vietnam, on the picket lines of a steel plant in Sheffield, or merely during the normative but oftentimes scary processes of moving from one life stage to another. That it took awhile for the film to catch on had more to do with failed marketing than a lack of resonance. That it tended to do better with youth involved the controversial, highly sexual nature of the subject matter.

It is also interesting to note the film's location. *Rocky Horror* is set in and around Denton, Ohio, a fictional, rural town in the upper Midwest. Denton was the setting used for the original London stage musical, and from its original title – *It Came From Denton High* – the narrative was clearly meant to be set in the United States due to the colloquial use of 'High' to denote secondary education. Furthermore, an official printed collection of materials involving the musical and film – *The Rocky Horror Scrapbook* (1998) – contains an address listing for Janet Weiss that reads, '10 Main Street, Denton, Ohio'. Despite the fact that we know very little about Denton, it appears to be a small town steeped in a golden past. A billboard promotes it as the 'Home of Happiness', although from what we see and hear and through the characters of Brad and Janet, Denton seems too good to be true during this time of increased political, economic and social complexity.

All things are constructs of the imagination, even towns, and in billing itself as the 'Home of Happiness' while adjacent to Frank-N-Furter's castle and its many perversions, *Rocky Horror* is reminiscent of another film released in 1975. In Steven Spielberg's *Jaws*, the town of Amity also has a small-town feel, a billboard constructing its own image (a bikini-clad girl reclining in the ocean on a body board, below the caption 'Amity Island Welcomes You') and a dark secret lying just below the surface. *Jaws* and *Rocky Horror* were at the forefront of a series of films that, over a period covering several decades, situated societal malaise within the breakdown of small towns and suburban spaces, including the following: *Edward Scissorhands* (Tim Burton, 1990), *Welcome to the Dollhouse* (Todd Solondz, 1995), *The Ice Storm* (Ang Lee, 1997), *American Beauty* (Sam Mendes, 1999), *Pleasantville* (Gary Ross, 1998) and *The Truman Show* (Peter Weir, 1998), the latter of which clearly owes a debt of gratitude to *Shock Treatment* (Jim Sharman, 1981), Richard O'Brien's sequel to *Rocky Horror*. In addition to its brief commentary upon small towns, the film's opening also pokes fun at institutions, including religion (churches filled for weddings and funerals but otherwise empty), marriage (Janet's immediate reaction to Brad's proposal involves the size of her ring *vis-à-vis* Betty's) and education (Ralph and Brad enter Dr Scott's class only to, respectively, woo Betty and Janet). Naturally, Brad and Janet are ignorant of these critiques, as they still live in a familiar, sheltered cocoon. As neither has yet lost their innocence, they have not been faced with the need for embracing the change or longing for the past. However, they are about to have their horizons broadened both suddenly and spectacularly.

Before they even reach Frank-N-Furter's castle, there are signs that they have forever left the cosy embrace of Denton and what it represents. Brad and Janet get lost in a thunderstorm, much as the United States was left politically adrift after the twin resignations of Vice President Spiro Agnew, for tax evasion and accepting bribes, and President Nixon, due to his role in covering up the Watergate scandal. Brad and Janet listening to Nixon's resignation speech as they lose their own way links their fall to the failures of western democracy, as for the first time in America's nearly (at that point) 200-year history, the President would be someone – Gerald Ford – who had never appeared upon a Presidential ticket, and therefore for whom the citizenry had not voted. Brad's statement about a motorcyclist who passes them – 'life's pretty cheap to that type' – illustrates the sheer distance from which he has allowed the mainstream culture to evolve beyond him. Much as the motorcyclist – notionally one of Frank's guests – overtakes Brad and Janet, so too have the times. Janet similarly performs the manner in which she is out of touch. She seeks to protect herself from the rain with a newspaper titled 'The Plain Dealer' (Cleveland, Ohio). Although likely this paper was chosen by the film's director and/or production designer in order to suggest an upper Midwest location, the title itself enjoys ironic properties. In a time typified by political infighting over aspects of both foreign (Vietnam War) and domestic policy (Civil Rights and the Great Society), and culminating in a presidential fall from grace when one political party was caught spying on another, hiding under 'The Plain Dealer' is a symbolic act of escapism out of touch with political realities. Furthermore, in singing the ballad 'There's a Light (Over at the Frankenstein Place)' shortly before marching off to lose her virginity

Mercy Killing: Rocky Horror, the Loss of Innocence
and the Death of Nostalgia
Andrew Howe

in remarkable fashion, Janet displays an optimism that is similarly misplaced. Within a few short hours, she will have had sexual intercourse with two different men, neither of whom are her fiancé. She does find a sort of enlightenment, true, but the light she finds within the castle is not at all what she expected.

Brad and Janet walk into a situation where self-indulgent excess and living in the moment are pursued while a much simpler past is simultaneously valorized. Such a schizophrenic approach to change is symptomatic of dual tendencies in the 1970s, a decade that saw a number of people revelling in new practices typified by the hedonistic mantra 'Sex, Drugs, and Rock & Roll' while simultaneously lionizing the past through rose-tinted glasses. The root of nostalgia is located in the latter, specifically in a personal and oftentimes absurdly exalted vision of the past and its notional superiority. As Dave Thompson notes in *Music on Film*, the post-World War II boom was the controlling factor in a generation of artists who came of age during the 1950s and who were beginning to produce their own art during a period of intense change:

Figure 2: Brad and Janet, as of yet unconvinced by Frank-N-Furter © Twentieth Century Fox.

> [P]eople in general, and artists in particular, were happier looking backward in time than forward to a future that could (and, pessimists delight, *would*) only get worse and worse. And the halcyon era, all seemed to agree, was the 1950s, those years when, with World War II won and a new affluence looming; with rock 'n' roll booming and Hollywood swinging; with science moving mountains and technology leaping over them, *anything* seemed possible.

Such nostalgia, however, often ignores or diminishes undercurrents of fear or repression that permeate any era. These undercurrents are often reflected in the cultural products of their time, case in point (for the 1950s): 'creature feature' films, with giant animals rampaging across the landscape indicative of the fear of atomic weaponry and a potential World War III.

Thus, not only was the response to popular culture in the 1970s schizophrenic, with many simultaneously celebrating the fruits of the present while they propped up the past, so too was the past divided between what actually transpired and what was remembered, either collectively or individually. Naturally, part of this schizophrenia was generational, although the popular culture of any era suggests that such a split between an allegiance to the past and an obsession with the present and future is natural. On the one hand, the numerous references to film and musical icons of the 1930s, 1940s and 1950s indicate nostalgia for a past that no longer exists. Steve Reeves and Buddy Holly were simpler stars for a simpler time, but those times have been washed away by the cultural and political upheavals that, naturally, impact the popular culture of the time. This is where the other part of the film's schizophrenia comes into play, as is evidenced upon first blush by the costuming of those in attendance at Frank's party. When Brad and Janet enter the mansion, they are drawn into a musical number that includes a bunch of

partygoers who look as if they are taking part in an Elton John lookalike contest. Throw in Frank's look, most likely inspired by David Bowie's early-1970s stage character Ziggy Stardust, and a decidedly androgynous element is introduced to the proceedings, one very much out of alignment with traditional notions of gender. It's as if Buck Rogers with his lantern jaw has given way to Major Tom and his prominent cheekbones. Using the popularity of *Rocky Horror* as a cultural barometer, western masculinity can be seen to have changed significantly or, at the very least, the impetus for change had increased, opening up new spaces for alternative gender identities.

The film's musings on transgression are not restricted to character costuming. The castle itself, its Gothic elements and the references to Transylvania seem stereotypical of how a conservative couple from middle America might view continental, aristocratic pleasure-seeking. Song lyrics and dialogue throughout the narrative reference specific aspects of hedonistic living, including both sex (the song lyric 'I don't want no dissension… just dynamic tension') and drugs (Riff waiting for the 'candy man', the song lyric 'You're spaced out on sensation, like you're under sedation'). It was no surprise then that when confronted with these elements, Brad and Janet first become unbalanced (he introduces her as 'Vice' instead of 'Weiss'; she keeps fainting) before succumbing to their inner desires. As becomes clear in their subsequent liaisons and in the song 'Creature of the Night', both have given themselves over fully to Frank's vision. They are not the only ones, however, as even Dr Scott, following a brief soliloquy about morality after the floorshow ('Fanfare/Don't Dream It, Be It'), discovers that he looks pretty good in silk stockings! However, as will be explored next with Frank's fall, this hedonistic approach is doomed to failure. The lyric holding up dynamic tension over dissension, sung by Frank, is particularly interesting coming during the politically and economically unstable times in which the film was released. One can only escape the world's problems for so long, and a programme of excess and self-indulgence if undertaken on a large scale will only enable such problems to grow worse.

There is only one character who bridges the need for change with a healthy vision of the past. Eddie is a throwback while simultaneously representing a figure of the counter-culture. As a rock-and-roll biker who has the courage (initially) to stand up for the past, Eddie represents a positive eruption of nostalgia in the midst of Frank's hedonistic project. Eddie interrupts the festivities aggressively, plays an old-time bluesy form of rock and roll on his saxophone, and stands (at least for a few minutes) as an alternative to Frank and his schizophrenic vision of the past.

Eddie proves weak, however, essentially letting Frank off him with an ice axe. Furthermore, the style of music coming in 1975 was well out of touch for the era. Buddy Holly had been dead for sixteen years and the British invasion had largely come and gone, with David Bowie, Freddie Mercury, Iggy Pop, Twisted Sister and other over-the-top icons of the glam-rock and shock-rock movements largely replacing them. Furthermore, this era also saw a developing musical aesthetic that would see the emergence of

Mercy Killing: Rocky Horror, the Loss of Innocence
and the Death of Nostalgia
Andrew Howe

punk rock with the Ramones in 1974 and the Sex Pistols in 1975. Out of this entire musical group, it was primarily glam rock and specifically David Bowie that most closely relates to the film and its success, as Dave Thompson notes in *Music on Film*:

> Its musical parameters notwithstanding, glam rock had just three fixations: sex, in as many varieties as could be found; science fiction, with as kitsch an angle as could be schemed; and a yearning nostalgia for the 1950s, when everything was simpler and tasted better too. *Rocky Horror* seized upon those same ingredients, inflated them beyond parody.

With the song 'Hat Patootie – Bless My Soul' and the character of Eddie, the film courts a narrative dissonance by setting what amounts to a traditional rock ballad on a stage, the design of which would be more at home at an Alice Cooper or K.I.S.S. concert. On the surface, Eddie seems as if he is the more legitimate character than Frank when it comes to merging the past with the present. However, the fact that he meets a quick demise and that the other characters literally consume him suggests that, figuratively, Eddie's project of nostalgia is one that is doomed to failure.

Figure 4: Eddie represents a brief counterpoint to Frank-N-Furter © Twentieth Century Fox.

The film's adherence to Frankenstein mythology extends beyond the notion of playing god, the problems inherent in the creative process or the aesthetic properties of mankind. The interplay of innocence and experience, and the subsequent musings upon morality and punishment, serve to situate the film within the Promethean tradition. In Greek mythology, Prometheus stole fire from Zeus so that mankind could benefit from this knowledge. As a result, he was condemned to eternal punishment by being tied to a rock and having his liver eaten daily by birds, only to have the organ regenerate for the morrow's feeding. Although Rocky is equivalent to Frankenstein's monster, Frank as a character represents a postmodern Prometheus. True to its schizophrenic nature, the film ends with multiple admonishments about morality, some of which contradict each other. After apparently being given control over their mission to earth, Riff kills Frank. It is more than just Frank's destruction, however, but the destruction of his hedonistic project, which Riff deems 'too extreme'. Dr Scott stops admiring his gams long enough to moralize about Frank's death sentence. However, at the same time the criminologist indicates to the audience that proper perspective is necessary: 'And crawling on the planet's face, some insects called the human race. Lost in time and lost in space and meaning'. The message appears to be: don't take yourself too seriously, as in the grander scheme of things the context upon which you place so much significance ultimately means very little. The song that accompanies the credits, however, undermines the criminologist's statement, returning to a more overtly and traditionally moral position as indicated by both Riff and Dr Scott. The lyric 'darkness has conquered Brad and Janet' suggests that the changes elicited within the couple by Frank are not only permanent – with their passage from inno-cence to experience irrevocable – but also immoral. In all of its various machinations, the ending simultaneously performs the death of innocence in the post-World War II period and the rejection of a hedonistic lifestyle that aspires to replace it. Although it may have equivocated a bit in the final frame, *Rocky Horror*'s relationship to societal trajectories since 1975 has indicated the triumph of its more progressive elements. Traditional models of patriarchy, monogamy and heterosexuality continue to crumble. Frank's project may have been 'too extreme' by Riff's standards, but Frank was on to something, and Brad and Janet will never again be the same. They have tasted the forbidden fruit and, as with the changing face of both the United States and the United Kingdom, there is no going back. One can celebrate the past, but allowing, through acts of nostalgia, prior codes of sexual or behavioural decorum to dictate contemporary morality will result in destruction. ●

GO FURTHER

Books

Music on Film: The Rocky Horror Picture Show
Dave Thompson
(Milwaukee: Limelight, 2012)

Rocky Horror: From Concept to Cult
Scott Michaels and David Evans
(London: Sanctuary, 2002)

Online

'Inside Rocky Horror'
Scott Miller
NewLineTheatre.com (n.d. [2002]), www.newlinetheatre.com/rockychapter.html.

'The Rocky Horror Picture Show and the Emergence of Recreational Evil.' *Transparency-Now.com* (n.d.), www.transparencynow.com/evil.htm.

Contributor Details

EDITOR

Marisa C. Hayes is a second-generation creature of the night specialized in dance films. Her French- and English-language publications are found in a variety of books and journals, including *The Oxford Handbook of Screendance Studies*, several volumes of Intellect's 'World Cinema' series, and the Society of Dance History Scholars' journal, *Conversations Across the Field of Dance Studies*, among others. She currently serves as co-director of the International Video Dance Festival of Burgundy in France. Other interests in the field of film and television studies have led to projects, such as guest-editing a recent television-themed issue of the journal *Supernatural Studies*. An avid traveller, Marisa enjoys being a culture vulture, watching all the old sci-fi films referenced in 'Science Fiction/Double Feature', and hanging out with a troupe of rescue cats and her husband.

CONTRIBUTORS

Franck Boulègue is a French film scholar and artist. Originally from Lyon, he earned a degree in political science and communication from the Institut d'Etudes Politiques and completed his graduate studies in communication at the University of Liverpool. He is a regular contributor to *Eclipses*, a French film-research journal for which he has analysed, among others, the filmographies of Tim Burton, Chris Marker and the Coen Brothers. His writing has also appeared in *Les Cahiers du Cinéma*'s book on Gus van Sant (2009). Franck co-edited the *Fan Phenomena: Twin Peaks* (Intellect, 2013) book with Marisa C. Hayes, as well as a new book about screendance entitled *Art in Motion* (Cambridge Scholars, 2015). He is currently writing a monograph about *Twin Peaks* for Intellect to be released in 2015 for the show's 25th anniversary.

Alissa Burger is Associate Professor at the State University of New York, Delhi where she teaches English and Humanities courses. She has taught courses in writing, film, literature and gender studies. Her research interests include representations of gender performativity in literature and film, revisionist literature, the role of the musical in contemporary popular culture, and the literary horror genre, with particular focus on Stephen King. She is the author of *The Wizard of Oz as American Myth: A Critical Study of Six Versions of the Story, 1900–2007* and editor of the collection *The Television World of Pushing Daisies: Critical Essays on the Bryan Fuller Series*.

Tara Chittenden is a qualitative researcher in the Research Unit of the Law Society in London. Her Ph.D. examined strategies used to interpret the body of a virtual-reality mummy displayed at the British Museum. Prior to her current employment, she worked at the British Museum and at Torquay Museum. Her research interests include practices of interpretation, teen identity formation, spatial narratives and technological interventions at museums and heritage sites. Recent publications have discussed the spectatorship of tennis fans at Wimbledon and female teens' emotional connection to a candy brand through the creation of Starburst Prom gowns.

Sarah Cleary is a final year Ph.D. candidate at Trinity College Dublin. For her doctorate, she is researching the role of the child in over 100 years of controversy surrounding the horror genre, across a range of mediums including films, comic books and video games. Combined with her studies, she tutors at Trinity College in Popular Literature. She has presented on horror, media manipulation, censorship and sexuality at numerous international conferences. She is a reviewer for the *Irish Journal of Gothic Horror* and will be published later this year in forthcoming publications on zombies, sexuality, fan culture, horror-related censorship and the films of Rob Zombie. In her spare time she has produced and acted in *The Rocky Horror Picture Show* in Dublin for almost a decade.

Shawn DeMille is a graduate student at San Francisco State University majoring in Linguistics. His main research focus is on multiple intersections of identity and how we use language to construct a multi-layered identity. He also has a strong interest in Corpus Linguistics, and has helped teach graduate-level seminars on the topic as well as presenting a paper on using *Friends* episodes to inform language teaching. He received his BA in English Language and Discourse from California State University, East Bay in 2008 and is heavily involved with higher education advocacy and policy development, utilizing some of his linguistic research to help prepare documents to influence policy changes.

Taos Glickman is a doctoral candidate at the University of Massachusetts, Amherst in the department of Communication. Her research focuses on youth, media literacy and identity. She is a native of Southern California, and received her BA from the University of California, Berkeley (2004); and MA from California State University, Los Angeles (2009). In addition to her scholarly pursuits, she has consistently worked with multicultural youth organizations in Boston, MA; Los Angeles, CA; and Oakland, CA.

Diana Heyne is an American multidisciplinary artist, arts writer and first-wave *Rocky Horror Picture Show* fan currently living in France.

Andrew Howe is Associate Professor of History at La Sierra University, where he teaches courses in film history and theory, popular culture and American history. Recent publications include articles on race and racism in *Star Wars* and the depiction of

Latino identity in *Breaking Bad*. Current research projects involve the rhetoric of fear employed during the 1980s killer bee invasions of the American Southwest, as well as the faith vs. science debate over the rediscovery of the Ivory-billed Woodpecker in Arkansas. These two works are conceived of as chapters in a book-length project exploring the manner in which societies translate environmental events by employing the familiar rhetorical strategies and vocabularies of existing, sociological problems.

Molly McCourt lost her *Rocky* virginity almost a decade ago one pleasurable night in the Union bar at Ohio University. Since then, she has experienced Dayton's first Annual Transylvanian Convention and looks forward to participating in the Sensual Daydreams midnight showing in Milwaukee. Currently, Molly is pursuing her Ph.D. in English at UW-Milwaukee in the Cinema, Media and Digital Studies track. While most of her research focuses on representations of masculinity in twenty-first-century film and TV, she credits Frank-N-Furter, the sweet transvestite himself, for sparking her fascination with gender performance early on in her studies.

Aubrey L. C. Mishou is an adjunct professor of English at the United States Naval Academy, and a Ph.D. candidate at Old Dominion University. A frequent conference participant, she most recently led a panel on 'Monstrous Maternity' at NeMLA 2014, where she also delivered a paper on the corpse of the sweetheart in Gothic fiction. Recent publications include '*The Hunger Games* and the Failure of Dystopian Maternity' (2013), 'Clothes Make the (Wo)Man: Eighteenth-Century Materialism and the Creation of the Female Subject' (2013) and 'Surviving Thornfield: *Jane Eyre* and Nineteenth Century Evolutionary Theory' (September 2014).

Reuben C. Oreffo, who comes from England, has worked as a language assistant and au pair in France. He is currently a student of philosophy at the University of Cambridge. In preparation for his degree, he explores philosophy independently with readings from Hume, Wittgenstein and Russell, inter alia. His principal philosophical interests are presently to be found in philosophy of language, general epistemology and formal logic, yet he has wider interests in those cases where philosophy can be found in conjunction with psychology or political theory. Other interests include choral music, Reuben having been awarded a choral scholarship to his Cambridge college of Corpus Christi.

Image Credits

From *The Rocky Horror Picture Show*

Chapter 1:   Figs 1-5
Chapter 2:   Figs 2-3
Chapter 3:   Figs 1, 3
Chapter 4:   Figs 1-3
Chapter 6:   Figs 1-6
Chapter 7:   Figs 1-6
Chapter 10: Figs 1-2, 4
© Twentieth Century Fox

From *Shock Treatment*

Chapter 8:   Figs. 1-5
© Twentieth Century Fox

Additional Images

Chapter 2:   Fig.1 © StatisSquareSpace
Chapter 2:   Fig.4 © Tumblr
Chapter 3:   Fig.2 © Tara Chittenden
Chapter 3:   Figs.4-5 © The Royal Mystic Order of Chaos/Robert Price
Chapter 4:   Fig.4 © ObviousMag.org
Chapter 4:   Fig.5 © Dayton's Annual Transylvania Convention
Chapter 5:   Figs. 1-2 © S. Baxter Cohen
Chapter 5:   Fig.3 © Jennifer Springel
Chapter 5:   Fig.4 © S. Baxter Cohen
Chapter 5:   Fig.5 © Ruth Fink-Winter
Chapter 9:   Figs. 1-6 © Hector Heathwood Photography
Chapter 10: Fig.3 © SammyDavisVintage
Fan Appreciation 3: © David Freeman
Fan Appreciation 4: © George of Midnight Madness
Fan Appreciation 6: © Kate Viezel

'DON'T DREAM IT, BE IT.'

FRANK-N-FURTER